I0540306

Inspire Me

Moments:

Living Out Loud with No Regrets

A. HARRIS BROWN

Published in the United States of America by:
A. B.etter Way Productions, LLC
www.AHarrisBrown.com

ISBN: 979-8-2186-8855-4

First Edition

For permissions, inquiries, or bulk purchases, please contact:
info@AHarrisBrown.com

Printed in the United States of America.

DEDICATION

To **Anthony II**, my greatest joy and the reason I push forward
every day.

To the memory of **my parents**, who shaped me, challenged me,
and loved me unconditionally.
Your lessons still guide me.

To **everyone who has ever felt unseen, unheard, or unworthy**,
this book is for you.

You are enough. You matter.

And to the **mentors, friends, educators, scholars and brothers
who have walked this journey with me**, lifting me up when I
couldn't see my own way forward.

Thank you.

TABLE OF CONTENTS

FOREWORD

A Word Before We Begin

Throughout life you will have many conversations with many people. For most people, those conversations will help shape who they are and more importantly who they decide to become. And who they become could, potentially, have a profound effect on how they perceive themselves and shape how they interact with the world.

But what if I told you that you will have far more conversations with yourself than you will ever have with all the people you communicate with combined? What if I told you that those conversations, the ones that you have with yourself, could be far more detrimental, depending on what kinds of conversations you are having with yourself, than you will ever have with someone else?

We, as humans, sometimes can be so hard on ourselves. We are far more critical of ourselves than the outside world. We also can be so cruel to ourselves that we sometimes can talk to ourselves about getting the most out of what life has to offer. But what if we were able to have a resource that helped us create a better dialogue with ourselves? What if we were able to tailor those conversations into something special that allowed us to get the most out of ourselves, and thus life itself?

Welcome to Inspire Me Moments, written by my brother Anthony H. Brown. Inspire Me Moments is a book that helps you with your inner self. Brown does a fantastic job at helping the reader have better conversations with themselves.

Brown uses his own life, and a resource, to help others deal with the development of understanding how critical it is that we are all nicer to ourselves. His book also serves as a workbook for the reader in asking the important questions to help shape a dialogue for getting what we want out of life.

Brown details the steps necessary to go from fears that all people have when dealing with their own anxiety and the person we all wish we could be. His step-by-step instructions builds and protects one's fragile insecurities until they are ready to bust out and yell at the world, "I am here! I am ready! I am amazing!"

Brown teaches the reader how to fall in love with himself. Once they love themself, they can love the world. They can live with no regret, and they can live with no fear. They can live with no fear of judgement, no fear of rejection and most importantly, they can live with no fear of failure.

Our time on Earth is precious. Brown's book Inspire Me Moments allows all of us to reach our full potential. He allows us to capture the essence of what being alive is all about. His willingness to use his own life gives everyone who reads Inspire Me Moments the permission to thrive in their own divine glory.

The book will have you shouting at the rooftops, "I too can be all I want to be!" And that is all anyone of us can ask for. So, start having better conversations with yourself so you too can reach for the stars. Being in love with yourself is not such a sad thing.

Brad J. Bowling
PRESIDENT, CODE MEDIA GROUP, LLC

PROLOGUE:
BEFORE THE BECOMING

From Clipboard to Calling

I didn't start this journey with a lesson plan. I didn't grow up dreaming of becoming a teacher. Truth be told, I thought my lane was somewhere between the stage, the studio, and the spotlight. But purpose has a way of finding you even when you don't know you're being followed.

It all shifted the day I stepped in as a substitute teacher for Dr. Clifford Wallace. Clipboard in hand, unsure of my next move, I was just trying to help out. But he saw something I hadn't yet claimed. He looked at me and said:

> *"You're already doing the work. You just haven't claimed the title."*

That moment became the seed that grew into a calling.

What you'll read in the pages ahead isn't just about education, it's about emergence.

Because before I ever stood in a classroom, I stood at a crossroads. I've lived with the silence of depression. I've felt the weight, both literal and emotional, of carrying 200+ extra pounds and pretending it didn't hurt.

I've navigated the grief of losing pieces of myself and the people I loved, wondering if healing would ever come.
And yet, here I am still becoming.

That's what this book is about. Not just inspiration, but transformation. Not just theory, but testimony.

Since that "clipboard moment," I've taught in the same halls that once raised me, stood beside the same educators who once poured into me, and coached students who reminded me of the version of myself still waiting to believe he belonged. I've learned that leadership isn't about perfection, it's about presence. That titles shift and roles evolve, but legacy lives in how we serve.

In this book, you'll meet the teachers and mentors who shaped me—like Mr. Al Patillo, the first Black male educator I ever had, whose quiet strength became my earliest model of culturally responsive leadership.

You'll witness the stories of students I've mentored, including one young man who didn't believe he was "college material" until we walked the journey together—and now he's mentoring students of his own.

You'll see the moments when I failed forward, when I stopped performing and started becoming.

And you'll meet the Guardian Sentinel—not just a character, but a metaphor for what it means to rise through the rubble and return as a protector, builder, and beacon for others.

You'll also hear about the days I didn't think I'd make it. About the moment I realized that surviving isn't the same as living. And about the decision to stop hiding—and start healing.

I've learned that education isn't just a job, it's sacred work. And the classroom? That's just one stage. I've taken this calling into community events, podcast studios, family engagement rooms, and national spaces—anywhere our stories deserve to be heard.

So, before you step into the first chapter, I want you to know something: You don't need to have it all figured out to begin. You just need to listen to what's pulling at your spirit. You just need to answer when your moment calls your name.

You may not have a title yet. But if you're here and reading this, questioning, stretching, and growing; let me tell you like Dr. Wallace told me, *"You're already doing the work."*

Now it's time to claim the life that's waiting for you on the other side of fear.

Education didn't just find me—I found myself through education.

This work has never just been about curriculum, it's about becoming.

That's what this book, this journey, and this calling has always been about.

Welcome to the journey.

Let's live it out loud—

With no regrets.

All heart.

HOW TO USE THIS BOOK

Your Guide to Healing, Reflection, & Growth

Inspire Me Moments: Living Out Loud with No Regrets is more than a memoir. It's a **mirror**, a **movement**, and a **map** for becoming. Whether you're a student finding your voice, an educator seeking deeper purpose, or simply someone walking through your own transformation, this book was designed to *walk with you*—not rush you.

You don't have to start at the beginning. **Flip to the chapter that speaks to your current season.** Whether it's grief, purpose, addiction, fatherhood, or forgiveness. Each chapter stands on its own and invites you to go deeper at your own pace.

Find the theme or subject that resonates with you, take a deep breath, and begin there. Here's how to make the most of your experience, individually or with others.

Read with Intention:

Each chapter offers raw reflection, life lessons, and soul-stirring calls to action. Take your time. Let the stories settle. Highlight what speaks to you. Revisit what challenges you.

Journey Through the Three Parts

The book is organized into **three transformational stages**:

Part I: Becoming

Theme: *Identity, self-worth, and courage to begin again.*

Chapter 1: The Moment, I Chose Me

Every hero's journey begins with a decision and this one starts in silence, in self-doubt, and in the shadows. But even quiet decisions can echo for a lifetime. In a world where hiding feels safer than healing, this chapter dares to step into the light. Through revelation and rupture, we witness the birth of a man who finally decided his life was worth living—and worth living out loud.

Subject Matter:

Depression	*Hope*	*Identity*
Self-Worth	*Silence*	

Chapter 2: The Cost of Carrying It All

What happens when the strong one breaks? When the mask slips, and the weight you carry becomes heavier than your will to keep going? This chapter peels back the layers of silent suffering, exploring the emotional toll of being everyone's anchor while drowning in your own storms. It's a gut-check on masculinity, vulnerability, and the quiet courage it takes to finally ask for help.

Subject Matter:

Anxiety	*Emotional Exhaustion*	
Masculinity	*Resilience*	*Vulnerability*

Chapter 3: Healing in Real Time

Healing isn't linear - and sometimes, it feels like bleeding in public. This chapter grips you by the collar and pulls you into the messy, glorious tension of restoration. As you confront relapse, resistance, and revelation, you're reminded that transformation doesn't come with a script. It comes with scars that become sacred roadmaps.

Subject Matter:

Divorce	*Fatherhood*	*Growth*	*Identity Crisis*
Mental Health		*Relapse*	*Sobriety*

Chapter 4: My Name is Victory

At the intersection of fear and faith, identity and healing, stands a name that was once whispered in uncertainty, now reclaimed in power. This is a testimony of survival and surrender, of scars that speak, and burdens finally released.

From a midnight scare to a mirror moment of truth. It's not just about what you've been called, it's about what you're willing to let go of to become who you were destined to be. Because real victory starts when we stop holding it in.

Subject Matter:

Acceptance	**Diagnosis**	**Faith**
Family	**Health Scare**	**Release**

Part II: Breaking Through

Theme: *Healing, resilience, redefining masculinity, and spiritual growth.*

Chapter 5: Rewriting the Narrative

Family isn't always where you find yourself and it's often where you first lose pieces of who you are. In this chapter, the past wrestles with the present in a battle of names, truths, and unspoken wounds. It's a deep personal excavation of identity beneath legacy, offering glimpses of healing where the fractures once lived. Prepare to question everything you thought you knew about belonging.

Subject Matter:

Abandonment	*Belonging*	*Family Trauma*
Generational Wounds		*Rediscovery*

Chapter 6: What Forgiveness Frees

Sometimes the hardest prison to escape is the one built by your own bitterness. This chapter is a reckoning with hurt, betrayal, and the long walk toward release. Through brutal honesty and soft revelation, you'll see that forgiveness isn't approval—it's survival. And what it frees isn't just the other person—it's you.

Subject Matter:

Emotional Healing	*Forgiveness*	*Grief*
Self-liberation	*Spiritual Release*	

Chapter 7: The Power of Brotherhood

In a world that often teaches men to go it alone, this chapter is a radical reminder that healing happens in community. Brotherhood isn't just about friendship–it's about accountability, vulnerability, and showing up for each other when it matters most. Through shared stories, sacred bonds, and iron-sharpens-iron moments, we see what's possible when men stop competing and start connecting. Real strength isn't found in isolation–it's forged in the fire of collective growth.

Subject Matter:

Brotherhood	*Community Support*	
Connection	*Mental Health*	*Trust*

Chapter 8: Walking in Your Purpose

Purpose may not arrive at the trumpet sound. However, it can show up in whispers and wondering. This chapter travels through sacred spaces, divine interruptions, and moments that appear ordinary until they're not. It asks what it really means to walk in purpose, not just talk about it. You'll be challenged to move, not because the path is clear, but because your calling is louder than your fear.

Subject Matter:

Divine Interruption	Faith	Identity
Mission	Purpose	

Part III: Building Beyond

Theme: *Purpose, legacy, leadership, and service.*

Chapter 9: The Power of Giving Back

Legacy isn't what you leave, it's what you live. This chapter shifts the spotlight from personal growth to communal impact, from elevation to expansion. You'll meet the people, places, and platforms that became the evidence of transformation in motion. Being perfect is not the goal. It's about passing the torch while it's still burning bright.

Subject Matter:

	Impact	Leadership	
Legacy in Motion		Philanthropy	Service

Chapter 10: The Power of Reflection

Sometimes the rearview mirror reveals more than the road ahead. In this chapter, time folds in on itself as the teacher becomes the student, and the lessons come full circle. It's a meditation on mentorship, memory, and the sacred duty of leading from the inside out. Reflection isn't nostalgia - it's how we make meaning of the miles we've walked.

Subject Matter:

Gratitude	Leadership	Legacy
Memory	Mentorship	

Chapter 11: Keep Walking, Keep Becoming

The cape was never the point; it was the preparation. This final chapter hands the pen to you, daring you to write the rest. The Guardian Sentinel steps aside, not to vanish but to remind you that becoming is a lifelong call. With fire in your bones and purpose in your step, you now carry what the world desperately needs: a life lived out loud, with no regrets.

Subject Matter:

Becoming	*Courage*	*Endurance*
Hope	*Next Chapter*	

Reflect Deeply

At the end of every chapter, you'll find:

- **Final Thought** – A closing reflection that captures the heart of the journey.
- **Inspire Me Moment** – A short affirmation with a QR code linking to a 1-minute video.
- **Live Out Loud Challenge** – A practical 3-part action: Connect. Reflect. Support.
- **Wellness Check-In** – A mind-body-soul activity to help you reset, grow, and breathe again.

These aren't "extras." They are *essential* to your journey. Use them. Revisit them. Share them with someone who needs them.

Use It with Your Circle

This book is *ideal* for:

- Book clubs
- Men's groups
- Faith-based small groups
- Counseling cohorts
- Staff or student leadership circles
- Community healing spaces

Each chapter stands alone for discussion – while also building a larger, life-giving arc. Use the chapter summaries to guide conversation starters or journaling prompts.

And if you're using this book with a group – invite me in. I'd be honored to join the conversation as an active listener, supporter, or special guest. Whether in person or virtually, your healing spaces matter, and I'd love to walk alongside you. You can reach out directly through my website: www.aharrisbrown.com

Join the Expanded Conversation

At the end of the chapter, scan the QR code to join **The Inner Circle Club.** This is a digital space for reflection, inspiration, and deeper community. You'll also find downloadable guides and updates to support your growth.

Make It Yours

Write in the margins. Journal your responses. Start conversations with your crew. This book is a guide and you're the author of what comes next.

You've named your truth—now dare to dream. Use this space to visualize the life you're creating. Who are you becoming? What does your future hold? Map it out here.

Vision Board

(Day): _____ *(Month):* _____ *(Year):* _____

(Remember)

CULTIVATING GRATITUDE IS A POWERFUL PRACTICE THAT CAN POSITIVELY IMPACT YOUR MINDSET AND OVERALL WELL-BEING. ENJOY THIS RITUAL, AND WATCH HOW IT CONTRIBUTES TO FULFILLED LIFE.

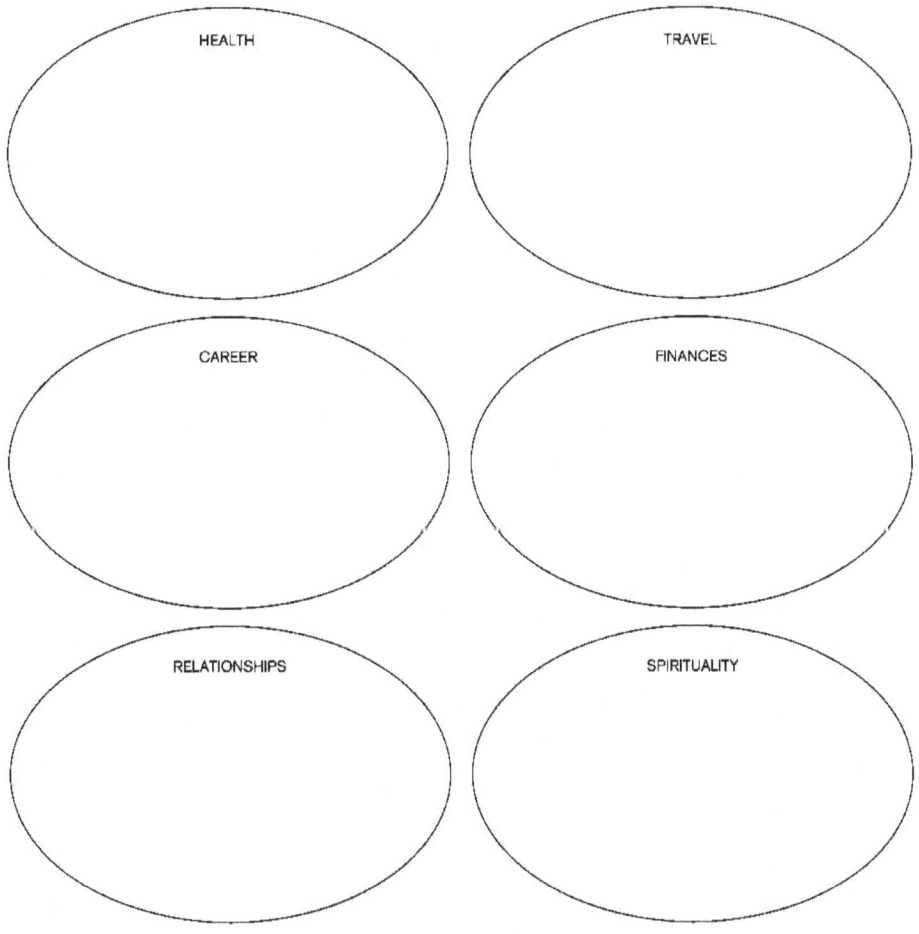

HEALTH

TRAVEL

CAREER

FINANCES

RELATIONSHIPS

SPIRITUALITY

PART I: BECOMING

Theme: Identity, self-worth, and courage to begin again

"Before you can build anything meaningful, you must first believe that you are worthy of the foundation."

This section invites readers to reflect on their earliest battles with self, with doubt, with identity and reminds them that healing begins with honesty.

There is always something to be thankful for. Even in the tension, there's a truth worth honoring. List what's bringing light to your life, no matter how small.

GRATITUDE JOURNAL

WEEK: MONTH: YEAR:

TODAY I'M GRATEFUL FOR

_____

_____

_____

_____

_____

SOMETHING
I'M PROUD OF

WORDS TO INSPIRE THE DAY

TODAY'S AFFIRMATION

_____

_____

_____

TOMORROW I LOOK FORWARD TO

WATER INTAKE

1L   2L   2.5L   3L

HOW HAVE I FELT THIS YEAR?

GOOD   NOT GOOD

CHAPTER 1:
THE MOMENT, I CHOSE ME

Opening Reflection

The stage is set: a young boy, eyes wide with wonder, flips through the pages of a comic book, finding solace in the tales of heroes who rise against the odds. In those vibrant panels, he sees not just capes and battles, but a reflection of his own yearning for purpose and belonging.

Fast forward, and that boy stands at a crossroads, burdened by self-doubt and the weight of expectations. The world has tried to dim his light, to confine him to the shadows of insecurity. But within him, a spark remains—a whisper that says, "Your story matters."

This chapter is the prologue to a journey of transformation. It's about embracing the hero within, stepping into the spotlight, and choosing to live out loud. Because the most compelling stories aren't just told, they're lived.

That spark I saw in comic books, you know the one that needs to be seen, to matter, to rise – never left me. It followed me into adulthood and into every room where I felt invisible.

Identity & Purpose

Why Not a Book

I never set out to write a book.

This entire journey, these Inspire Me Moments, the Walking Ministry, the conversations, the reflections—started as something deeply personal. A way for me to process, to release, to walk through life's challenges one step at a time.

But then one day, a teacher colleague, Audra Woods, pulled me aside. She had been following my videos and reflections. She saw the storytelling, the layers, the depth. And then she said something that stuck with me:

"There is no testimony without a test, and others could learn from these life lessons."

I laughed. I shook my head. *Why?* I thought. *Why would anyone want to read about my journey?*

And then she simply responded, "Why not?"

That was the moment. The spark that lit the match.

She was right. I do have a story. You have a story. We all have a story. And if one moment, one reflection, one affirmation in these pages can encourage just one person – then this book has done its job.

This is not just a book of affirmations. It's not just a memoir. It's not just a collection of thoughts and experiences.

This is a journey.

A journey of growth, self-reflection, purpose, and becoming.

And I hope that somewhere along the way, you find pieces of yourself in these pages.

Living Out Loud with No Regrets

For so long, though I was a big guy, 450 pounds at my heaviest—I played small. I hid parts of myself. I felt ashamed of my struggles, my weight, my insecurities. I questioned if I was good enough, worthy enough, or if I even belonged.

I made myself smaller in rooms where I should have taken up space.

I held my voice back when I should have spoken.

I laughed off pain that I should have confronted.

And here's an interesting note about me:

I wasn't always the biggest fan of reading.

But then, somewhere and somehow, I got my hands on my first Superman comic book as a child.

And that changed everything.

It wasn't just about the heroics or the action-packed pages—it was about what Superman represented.

He was different. He stood for something bigger than himself. And despite his alien origin, he dedicated his life to doing good, making a difference, and being a beacon of hope. That story stayed with me. Looking back, I see now that Superman wasn't just a character. I was projecting my hope through his belief system. And slowly, I began to build a version of that hero in my own reflection.

Somewhere between my childhood love of comic books and the reality of my own struggles, I really took to reading. It became my escape—a way to see myself differently, to believe in something greater. And on that journey of self-discovery, I realized something: We all have a hero inside of us.

It was through this connected universe of heroes that I shaped my belief that there is good in all of us, and with a little HOPE, life can be better.

I think I always had this thought that if I woke up every day with an "S" on my chest, I could save the world somehow.

But first—I had no idea that I would need to save myself. That's the real journey.

Guardian Sentinel: The Hero Within

For me I became, Guardian Sentinel. He stands for the best version of myself. The part of me that rises above. That part that fights for equity and justice. The part that discerns the right path forward even when the way is unclear.

His presence, in this book, is not obvious—you won't find a chapter dedicated to his story. But if you pay close attention, you will see him. You will feel him. Because he is all of us. He is you when you make the hard choice to stand up for yourself.

He is you when you push past fear and take that first step toward change. He is you when you fight for something bigger than yourself.

And if he had just one piece of advice for you, it would be this:

> *"Mistakes will be made. But what's to come is still better than what has been."*

That's where Guardian Sentinel was born—not in fantasy, but in the real decision to fight for myself and others when it would've been easier to disappear.

What Living Out Loud Really Means

"Living Out Loud" is not about volume—it's about presence.

It's about showing up fully—flaws, quirks, passions, and all.

It's about owning your voice, your past, and your future.

No longer would I allow insecurity to dictate my steps.

No longer would I let fear of judgment silence me.

No longer would I dim my own light for the comfort of others.

Now, I live. I walk. I speak. I inspire.

I embrace every part of who I am—because I refuse to live a life of regret.

Reflection is the Key

Life moves fast.

It's easy to get caught up in the daily grind, to keep pushing forward without ever stopping to ask:

- How did I get here?
- Where am I going?

- Who am I becoming?

That's why reflection is so powerful.

It allows us to step back, to see the bigger picture, to learn from the lessons that life is constantly trying to teach us. But even more than reflection, writing became a mirror. It didn't just help me heal; it helped me find my voice.

Through the Inspire Me Moments in this book, you'll find reflections on growth, resilience, faith, struggle, and victory. You'll see raw, unfiltered stories that showcase both the highs and the lows— because true transformation happens in both.

I hope that as you read, you take time to pause, to sit with the words, and to ask yourself:

- What does this mean for me?
- How can I apply this to my own life?
- What changes am I willing to make?

Writing With Purpose

I almost did not write this book. I almost let self-doubt and perfectionism talk me out of completing this project.

I almost convinced myself that my story did not matter.

But then, I remembered—this book is not just for me.

It's for you.

It's for anyone who has ever felt defeated.

For anyone who has ever thought they weren't enough.

For anyone who has ever felt different, out of place, unseen, unheard.

This book is for dreamers.

For the fighters.

For the ones who are still figuring it out but refuse to give up.

And if there's one thing, I hope you take away from these pages, it's this:

You belong.

You matter.

Your story is worth telling.

Now, let's walk this journey together.

"Dear Me" A Letter to the Boy Who Needed to Hear This

But before we go forward, allow me to go back. Back to the boy who needed this book long before I ever wrote it.

Dear Me,

I know you're struggling. I can feel the weight on your shoulders, the insecurities gnawing at your confidence, and the self-doubt that seems to follow you around like a shadow. You've already been through a lot—loss, pain, and moments where you felt invisible. But here's the truth: you are more than you think. And in the years to come, you'll realize that your journey has a purpose far greater than what you can see right now.

I see you, trying to fit in, trying to be accepted, trying to find your way in a world that often feels so confusing. I see you running from your own struggles because facing them feels too overwhelming. But you must know this: it's okay to be different. It's okay to feel lost at times. But don't let those moments define you. They don't have the power to break you unless you allow them to.

You're at a point where you'll start to question who you are and if you matter. There will be times when you will doubt your worth. You'll look in the mirror and wonder if you're good enough. But I want you to know this now—you are enough. Not because of the weight you carry, or the things you've accomplished, but because of who you are at your core.

You will go through periods of immense growth and hardship. You'll face battles with weight, both physical and emotional, and you'll struggle with unhealthy habits that will take a toll on your mind and spirit. You'll often feel like you're not enough, like you're carrying the world on your shoulders. But know this, you won't always feel this way. Your strength will grow, your confidence will blossom, and you'll learn to love yourself in ways you can't even imagine right now.

There will be moments when you will look at your life and feel overwhelmed. But hold on to this truth: every setback is a setup for a comeback. You'll face your demons, but in doing so, you will discover a strength within you that will propel you forward. Every failure will teach you something; every misstep will lead you to a better path.

There will come a time when you learn to embrace your struggles instead of running from them. You'll realize that they are not your enemy, but your teachers. You'll understand that the pain you've felt will be the very thing that propels you toward greatness. And when you reach that place, you'll look back at the boy you once were and say, "You did it. You made it through."

I'm proud of you, even when you don't see progress. I'm proud of your resilience, your courage to keep going even when life gets tough. And I want you to know—this is just the beginning.

So, don't rush it. Don't try to be perfect. Don't try to fit into someone else's mold. Embrace who you are. Embrace your story. And when the world tries to tell you who you should be, stand firm in who you already are.

The world will see you eventually. But first, you must see yourself. With love and understanding,

Your Future Self

Final Thought: Living Out Loud with Purpose

Life is a journey filled with challenges and opportunities to grow. The key to transformation is embracing who you are, flaws and all, and taking intentional steps forward.

How often do you let past mistakes or failures define your present moment?

_____

_____

_____

What would it look like to fully embrace who you are and walk through the world with purpose and confidence?

_____

_____

_____

How can you build a life of meaning by connecting with the right people, reflecting on your growth, and supporting others on their journey?

_____

_____

_____

Embrace the journey. Take the next step. And know that you are not alone. Let's walk this journey together.

Inspire Me Moment: A Confidant

No one should have to carry his or her burdens alone. Having a trusted confidant—someone to listen without judgment—can make all the difference. As you continue your journey, think about who has been there for you and how you can be that person for someone else.

"Sometimes you simply need someone kind to sit with you while you deal with things."
Gail Honeyman

Reflection:

In life's toughest moments, having a kind soul by your side can work wonders. Not every problem needs a solution, and not every struggle needs a speech. Sometimes, you just need someone to sit with you—in the silence, in the storm—and simply be present.

The power of human connection and companionship should never be underestimated. A confidant doesn't have to fix your problems, their presence alone can provide immense comfort, reminding you that you're not alone.

Take a moment to reflect: **Who has been that person for you? And just as importantly, whose burden are you willing to share?**

Final Thought:

Everyone deserves someone who simply listens. **Be the kind of confidant whose presence speaks louder than words.**

Live Out Loud Challenge:
A Confidant

True strength isn't found in isolation. It's built in safe, trusted spaces. This challenge reminds you to honor those who held space for you, reflect on the power of trust, and be that anchor for someone else.

Connect

Reach out to someone who showed up for you in a pivotal moment. Remind them of their impact with a simple message: *"Your presence mattered more than you know."*

Reflect

With a trusted friend, mentor, or peer, discuss: What makes someone a safe space? What qualities create real trust? Reflect on how you've been both the seeker and the shelter in different seasons of your life.

Support

Check in with someone newer on their journey—whether younger in age, experience, or spirit. Don't fix it. Don't preach. Just show up and listen. Your presence alone can be the lifeline they didn't know they needed.

Wellness Check-In
The Journey to Living Out Loud

Purpose: Embrace your identity, stand tall in your truth, and visualize your next bold step forward.

◇ **3 Actions**

1. **Visualize** your future self—5 years from now. Where are you? What do you feel like?

2. **Stand tall.** Ground yourself with your feet firm, fists clenched, then released. Repeat: "I stand strong in my purpose."

3. **Affirm aloud:** "I am bold, I am strong, and I walk in my purpose with confidence."

◇ **2 Reflection Prompts**

- What part of your future self excites you the most?

- When have you stood firm in your identity, even when it was hard?

◇ **1 Final Word**

Live out loud. Your voice matters. So does your presence. Take one unapologetic step this week toward who you are becoming.

The Inner Circle Club

**You've just stepped through something powerful.
Now it's time to speak on it and allow your "NET" Work!**

This is your space to connect, reflect, and build community with other readers.

CHAPTER 1: The Moment, I Chose Me

- What's one moment in your life when you finally choose yourself?

- When did you realize your story was worth telling?

- What fears still try to dim your light—and how are you pushing through?

CHAPTER 2:
THE COST OF CARRYING IT ALL

Opening Reflection

Some weight is visible—heavy bags, sagging shoulders, tired eyes. But the heaviest weight? It's the one nobody sees. It's the regret we tuck into briefcases, the shame stitched into suits, the grief hidden behind polished smiles.

Every step forward can feel like dragging a thousand yesterdays behind you. Every new morning can feel like a silent negotiation with old pain:

"Can I let it go today? Will it follow me anyway?"

We don't realize how much we're carrying until one day, something—or someone—whispers, "Put it down." And maybe, for the first time, we actually listen.

This chapter isn't just about the weight we hold. It's about learning to name it. Face it. Then lay it down. And maybe, just maybe, you will be able to spread your wings again. The weight will always try to follow you. But freedom starts when you decide it doesn't get to ride on your back anymore.

Letting Go of What We No Longer Need

Yesterday's Weight

Life is a funny thing. We spend so much time stressing, worrying, and agonizing over the weight of yesterday. But here's the thing: Yesterday is gone. It's behind us, and we have a new opportunity today. That's right—today is a new day, and it comes with new opportunities. What happened yesterday happened, but holding onto it doesn't serve us. Looking back is one thing, staying there is something else.

While working at a particular high school, I would take my usual morning walk before school starts. And just like clockwork I would see my morning companion goose. I would swear this is the same goose I see every day. Same time. Same place. Watching.

And then, just like every day, it took off—seemingly unbothered, and unburdened.

I can only imagine that it doesn't carry yesterday when taking flight. It doesn't stop mid-flight, looking back at the ground like, *"Did I mess up yesterday? Did I fly the wrong way?"* No. It just flies.

As I walked, I thought about how often we let things linger. Such things as that fight from yesterday, that stress from work, that fear of what's next, weighs us down. And before we know it, we're walking into today already defeated by yesterday. So, I wonder, does that goose have the same kinds of concerns?

Sometimes, it feels like we're carrying more weight than we can bear. And sometimes, we spend way too much time rehashing our failures, disappointments, and regrets. This weight doesn't just sit in our minds—it creeps into our mornings, sits in our coffee cups, and settles into our bones. But we don't have to let that happen. We can choose to put it down.

Some days are heavier than others. We feel like we're pushing against something unseen. It can feel like the world is stacking everything on top of us, daring us to buckle. Yesterday was one of those days. But today? Today, I decided to put it down.

But deciding to put it down is one thing. Learning how to release it? That's the real work.

The Struggle with Letting Go

I've carried a lot of emotional baggage over the years.

- The hurt from church.
- The hurt from my dad.
- The hurt from my ex-wife.
- The hurt from losing jobs.
- The hurt from bad relationships.

It was all part of my emotional suitcase, and it was weighing me down. I had to stop and ask myself: Why was I still holding onto things that weren't serving me? Why was I keeping all this baggage? It was like putting bricks in a suitcase—making it heavier with each step I took. And sometimes, I didn't even realize how much I was carrying until someone I loved handed me the truth.

A good friend of mine said it best:
"Put it down." And I heard it.
I realized that holding onto yesterday's pain, regrets, and mistakes wasn't helping me. It wasn't pushing me forward. If anything, it was anchoring me in the past.

Like that goose I saw every morning when I was walking. Every day, that bird was there, standing in the same spot, doing its thing. Using my sanctified imagination, it didn't seem weighed down by yesterday. And in a moment, it just flew. And that's what I needed to do—stop carrying yesterday with me and just fly.

It was difficult, letting go of what no longer served me. Pain, shame, guilt, the weight of old versions of me—they were all still sitting in that metaphorical backpack. Some things I placed in there. Others were packed in by people and moments that shaped me long ago. For a long time, I thought I could manage everything on my own. I truly believed that asking for help – or even feeling the hurt – was weakness. But as Brené Brown (2012) puts it in *Daring Greatly*,

> ➤ *"Vulnerability is the birthplace of love, belonging, joy, courage, empathy, and creativity."*

What I once saw as weakness—letting people see me struggle—was actually the gateway to real connection. That backpack wasn't just full of weight; it was full of stories I hadn't yet dared to tell.

Letting go wasn't just about leaving behind the hurt. It was also about learning to forgive myself. The guilt, shame, and regret had no place in my present. I needed to make room for peace, for growth, for the future. And just when I thought I had unpacked it all, a conversation with a brother brought it home in the simplest, most powerful way.

Man Put It Down

I'll never forget a conversation I had with my brother Kevin Allen one morning. We were talking about the struggles we face when carrying the weight of the past, and Kevin said something that stopped me in my tracks:

> *"Man, we got to put it down. Whatever you carry, it's only as heavy as you let it be."*

His words echoed in my spirit, but I knew this wasn't a solo assignment. Healing needed backup. Kevin wasn't just talking about physical weight—he was naming emotional, mental, and spiritual burdens. It's the kind of weight we carry so long, we forget what it feels like to live without it. And here's another truth: many men never do. According to the American Foundation for Suicide Prevention, men die by suicide nearly four times more often than women. The emotional weight we carry in silence too often becomes fatal.

> *"Come to me, all you who are weary and burdened, and I will give you rest."* — **Matthew 11:28**

That scripture pierced through my soul like fresh air. I had been weary—not just in my body, but in my bones, my mind, my spirit. For the first time, I heard that verse not as a religious phrase, but as a personal invitation. A call to lay it down.

The Power of Support

Letting go is hard on your own. That's why I believe in the power of a strong support system. I didn't do it alone. My faith, my community, and my family helped me. Being vulnerable and connecting with the right people was key to moving forward.

One of the most important things I've learned is that vulnerability is crucial. When you let others into your pain, they don't use it against you—they help you work through it. My support system reminded me that it's okay to not have all the answers, to not be perfect. Sometimes, just having someone listen and say, "It's okay to struggle, it's okay to feel," gets you through the hardest times. Letting go doesn't happen overnight. It's a process.

I had to face the truth that I couldn't do this alone. I sought help. I got professional support. I built healthier habits. Therapy, medication, and journaling became part of my daily routine. It wasn't easy—but it was necessary.

Sometimes I like to say that my therapy sessions, my meds, and my journal entries are my "happy pills" now—not "crazy pills." It was a mental shift in how I saw myself and my healing journey. Every day, I worked on shedding the weight of the past and investing in a mindset that made space for joy.

It took time. But each day, I chose to show up. I chose to let go. And in doing so, I finally started to live without the burden of the past holding me back. The past no longer defined me—but there was still more to discover. Especially about where I came from, and who I was becoming next.

Final Thought: The Power of Letting Go

Life is full of challenges and burdens, but the key to moving forward is letting go of the weight you don't need. It's time to stop carrying yesterday's baggage into today.

What emotional baggage are you still holding onto that's weighing you down?

_____

_____

_____

What would happen if you finally let it go and embraced today?

_____

_____

_____

How can you move forward by choosing to release what no longer serves you?

_____

_____

_____

It's time to put it down. Move on and let go. And let's walk through it together.

The Reset: Walking Toward a New Life

Realizing the Need for Change

Recovery is something else. That's all I could think about during one of my toughest seasons. There was a time when I thought that just showing up for others would be enough to carry me through life. I focused on helping my mother, father, students, and my community, thinking that if I was present for them, I was doing okay. But the truth? I wasn't okay.

In my own body, the signs were clear: at my heaviest I weighed 450 pounds. My health was a ticking time bomb, and I couldn't ignore it any longer. But here's the kicker—it wasn't just about the weight. It was everything that came with it: years of stress, emotional baggage, and a deep internal struggle that I had been running from.

The words my father spoke echoed in my mind like a thunderclap:

- Did I really want my son to carry this burden one day?
- Did I want him to watch me struggle; the same way I had watched my parents?
- What kind of example was I setting?

And at that moment, I realized something had to change. It wasn't just about the physical transformation, it was about the emotional, mental, and spiritual healing I had been avoiding. I knew I couldn't continue down the path I was on, and I had to decide for my future, for my son's future, and for my legacy. That realization didn't come out of nowhere. It was built over time, moment by moment, mirror by mirror, warning by warning.

The Catalyst: A Wake-Up Call

My health journey was never a straight path. It took one big wake-up call to make me realize that something had to change. It wasn't a single moment; it was a collection of them that led me to the decision to press the reset button. My weight had been spiraling out of control, and the effects were undeniable.

I remember one particularly crushing moment: standing in front of a mirror, breathing heavily, seeing a man who had lost himself. And then it hit me—my son deserved better. I didn't want him to live through what I had lived through. I didn't want him to have to take care of me in my old age, burdened by a lifetime of my bad decisions. That was when I made the commitment to change. But commitment alone isn't transformation. Change happens in the trenches. Step by step, breath by breath.

Recovery: The Journey to Self-Healing

After that wake-up call, things began to shift. The first thing I did was make the decision to stop drinking alcohol. The emotional weight I had been carrying for years started to surface. It wasn't easy, but I knew it was necessary.

I also started walking. Slowly at first, just a few minutes here and there. But each step was a commitment to me. A promise to do better. I wasn't perfect, and I didn't expect it to be. But every day, I made progress. I embraced the journey, even when it was tough. I could barely make it around the block. But with every step, I felt myself getting stronger, even when my body screamed in pain.

And when the day came for me to undergo gastric bypass weight loss surgery, I was ready. I didn't see it as a quick fix, but as a tool— just another resource to support the change I was working toward. This wasn't about the surgery. For me, undergoing gastric bypass surgery was a decision rooted in the desire to live a healthier life. My health was deteriorating rapidly. I had been struggling with various health issues, sleep apnea, high blood pressure, and chronic pain — which all pointed to the fact that I needed a life-changing decision.

You also must understand that this wasn't my first attempt to journey down this surgery path. I had seen some level of success from friends and close family—people I loved and trusted who had made the leap and were experiencing visible change. And I wanted that too. I thought I could do this as well, but here's the truth: I was chasing the outcome, not the process. I wasn't mentally prepared for what was truly at stake. I didn't grasp the depth of what this decision needed.

At that time, it was all about appearance for me. I saw the procedure as a shortcut—cosmetic surgery that would make me look slim and trim, quickly. I didn't take the time to understand that weight loss surgery is not a magic fix. I ignored the deeper emotional and psychological layers—the food triggers, the trauma, the habits, the healing—that had to be addressed before real change could happen.

I thought looking better would make everything better. But I was trying to fix an internal struggle with an external solution—and that never works. But looking back, I realize now that mindset is everything. I hadn't done the internal work. I wasn't honest with myself, and I wasn't ready to commit to the lifelong transformation it demanded. So, when it didn't happen the way I imagined—or as fast as I thought—I gave up.

That failed attempt taught me something critical: timing and intention matter. Just because a door is available doesn't mean you're ready to walk through it. I had to grow. I had to mature emotionally and spiritually. I had to learn that this journey wasn't about shrinking my body—it was about expanding my life.

But when I finally made the decision to undergo surgery, it wasn't just about addressing my physical health concerns—it was about making a true commitment to me, my family, and my future. It was about choosing life, not only for myself, but for my son and the legacy I wanted to leave behind. The surgery became a tool that helped me reset my life, offer an ongoing support, provide a shift in my mindset, and the aid in the dedication to a healthier lifestyle that truly made the difference.

And for those unfamiliar with what this process truly involves, here's a closer look at the tool that helped support my transformation.

Understanding Gastric Bypass Surgery: A Tool for Change

Gastric bypass surgery, also known as Roux-en-Y gastric bypass, is a type of weight loss surgery designed to help people who are severely obese lose weight by making changes to their digestive system. The procedure involves two main components:

- ➢ Creating a Small Stomach Pouch: The surgeon reduces the size of the stomach to about the size of an egg, which significantly limits the amount of food the stomach can hold.
- ➢ Re-routing the Small Intestine: The surgeon connects the small stomach pouch to the lower section of the small intestine, bypassing part of the stomach and the upper intestine (duodenum). This limits calorie and nutrient absorption, leading to weight loss.

Gastric bypass surgery is typically recommended for individuals with a Body Mass Index (BMI) of 40 or higher, or a BMI of 35 or higher with obesity-related conditions such as type 2 diabetes, high blood pressure, or sleep apnea.

Source: Mayo Clinic Staff. (2024). Gastric Bypass (Roux-en-Y). Mayo Clinic.

Recovery and Lifestyle Changes After Surgery

While gastric bypass surgery is a powerful tool for weight loss, it's important to note that it is not a quick fix. The surgery is just one part of a long-term process that requires dedication and significant lifestyle changes. Patients must follow a specific diet and exercise regimen, take vitamin supplements to avoid nutritional deficiencies, and keep regular follow-up appointments with their healthcare providers.

The Importance of Choosing the Right Approach

Gastric bypass surgery isn't for everyone, and it's essential to make an informed decision with guidance from medical professionals. It's a long-term commitment to health and well-being. For me, it was the beginning of a healthier future, and it taught me one crucial lesson: Life is about making the right decisions, and the strength to change comes from within. But knowing that doesn't make the process any easier. The real work? It began in the days that followed.

The Struggle: Fighting Through Pain

The recovery process was grueling. The physical pain was almost unbearable, but the real battle was mental. I had to rebuild not just my body, but my mindset. I had moments when I felt like giving up—when I questioned if the pain was worth it. But I remembered my "why." I remembered why I started.

I had to find the courage to keep moving forward, to keep walking through the pain. And every day, it got a little easier. Every small win, every step forward, was a victory. I was not the same person I had been before. And with every step, I knew I was getting closer to the man I wanted to be.

The Reset Button: A New Perspective on Life

Surgery was only part of the equation. The real transformation happened when I committed to making my life a priority. I became consistent in my efforts—walking, eating right, and focusing on my mental and emotional health. I had to reset my entire outlook on life. I no longer wanted to live in the shadows of my past mistakes. One of the biggest lessons I learned through this journey is now I eat to live instead of loving to eat.

Now, when I look at myself, I don't see a man weighed down by his past. I see someone who fought to change, who pressed reset, and who chose to live life differently. I'm not perfect, but I'm better. I'm healthier, I'm stronger, and I'm more present in my son's life. That's the legacy I want to leave for him. Still, even with a new mindset, I couldn't walk this path alone. I needed people. I needed community.

The Community: Strength in Support

Another lesson learned is the importance of support. I didn't do this alone. My family, my community, and my faith have all been instrumental in helping me get to where I am today. There were times when I wanted to quit, but it was the encouragement from others that kept me going.

I also found a support group in the hospital and an online community of people who were going through the same struggles and achievements from weight loss surgery. We shared our experiences, our triumphs, and our setbacks. In those moments, I realized that I wasn't alone. There's strength in community, and there's even greater strength in vulnerability.

The Role of Faith: Trusting the Process and the Power of Belief

As I began my physical transformation, I faced not just the struggle with my weight and health but also the spiritual testing that came with it. I had always been a man of faith, but this journey—this battle to reclaim my life—put my faith to the ultimate test. There were days when I questioned if I was on the right path, moments when I doubted if I could really change, moments when I wondered if I was doing enough. I'd pray for strength and clarity, but the road was still tough, and sometimes, the answers didn't come as quickly as I wanted them to.

But then, I remembered the words of a song that always stuck with me,

> *"If your faith is strong enough, if you keep believing long enough, if you sing God's song enough, your faith will set you free."*

At some point, I realized that this journey was more than just about losing weight—it was about trusting God's plan for me, even when I couldn't see the way forward.

I was forced to live in the tension of doubt and belief. There were days when my faith was tested. But with every challenge, I reminded myself that if God had brought me this far, He would see me all the way through. I had to learn to trust in the process, even when it seemed slow or uncertain. And that trust was not just in the physical transformation, but in the spiritual growth I was experiencing alongside it.

Faith was the anchor that kept me grounded during the most difficult days, and that foundation became my strength. It wasn't a quick fix, but faith, in tandem with the physical and mental effort I was putting in, began to shift the trajectory of my life.

By trusting God's plan, I started to believe in myself again. And every step, every victory—no matter how small—was a reminder that God was walking with me through this journey, helping me navigate my struggles. And while the road isn't finished, I've come far enough to see what's waiting ahead—hope, purpose, and a future I never imagined.

The Future: A New Chapter

As I continue this journey, I know I have a long road ahead of me—but I also know I'm built for it. I'm no longer carrying the weight of who I used to be. The future is open, and I'm walking toward it with clarity, one step at a time.

There are still tough days, but I've learned that progress isn't about perfection—it's about showing up, choosing growth, and moving forward with intention. I've let go of shame, embraced grace, and started walking in freedom.

This isn't the end of my story—it's a new beginning. And this time, I'm not just surviving, I'm living. With purpose. With faith. With power.

Final Thought: Embrace the Journey of Transformation

Recovery is not just about overcoming the struggles of yesterday. It's about finding the strength to move forward. Each day is an opportunity to reset, to grow, and to transform in ways we never thought possible.

What parts of your life are you ready to reset and let go of?

_____

_____

_____

How can you trust the process, even when the answers don't come as quickly as you want them to?

_____

_____

_____

What step can you take today to reclaim your health, your happiness, and your purpose?

_____

_____

_____

Transformation takes time, but the first step is yours to take. Don't let fear or doubt hold you back. Embrace your journey, your future is waiting.

Inspire Me Moment:
From Darkness

We don't just grow from the easy moments—we grow through the struggles, the setbacks, and the seasons of uncertainty. The weight we carry can feel overwhelming at times, but even in darkness, there is transformation. Take a moment to sit with this truth before moving forward.

> *"All the variety, all the charm, all the beauty of life*
> *are made up of light and shade."*
> Leo Tolstoy

Reflection:

Think about the darkness you've faced—those moments that felt like they might break you. And yet, here you are, still standing. The beauty of life isn't just in the highlights, but in the shadows too. Those hard times helped shape you.

You didn't just survive; you grew. Every setback was part of the blueprint that made you stronger and wiser. Often, it's the struggle that leads to our deepest transformation.

You're not here by accident. Even in your darkest moments, change was happening. And now, you are proof of the strength that rises when you refuse to give up.

Final Thought:

Darkness isn't the end—it's the beginning of a transformation. From every shadow comes a clearer understanding of who you are and who you're becoming. Don't fear the hard seasons. They're shaping the strength you'll need for what's next.

Live Out Loud Challenge:
From Darkness

Darkness doesn't last forever and often, it's where our deepest growth begins. This challenge is about holding space for pain, honoring resilience, and helping others find their way toward the light.

Connect

Reach out to an elder, mentor, or trusted friend who has weathered a major storm. Ask them: *"What helped you find your light when things felt darkest? What did you hold onto that kept you moving?"*

Reflect

With a trusted peer, revisit a challenging season you've both experienced. Reflect together: *"How did that struggle shape who we are today? What hidden strength did we uncover in the process?"*

Support

Reach out to someone younger or newer in their journey who might be carrying silent burdens. Let your story be a light: *"Even in the dark, you're growing. Even in the struggle, strength is forming. Your light is coming—and you're not alone."*

Wellness Check-In
The Weight We Carry

Purpose: This check-in guides you through the process of releasing emotional burdens by spiraling inward with honesty and outward with clarity so you can walk forward feeling lighter and freer.

Reflection Spiral

1. What am I carrying?

Name one emotional burden—guilt, regret, fear, resentment. Write it down or say it aloud. Acknowledge its weight.

2. Where did it come from?

Trace the source. Was it something someone said? A past failure? An unspoken fear? Honor the origin without judgment.

3. What has it taught me?

Consider the lesson within the pain. What has carried this weight revealed about your strength, your values, or your boundaries?

4. What am I ready to release?

Choose what no longer serves you. Breathe it out. Stretch it out. Wash it off. Say: *"I do not have to carry this anymore."*

5. What am I creating space for?

Visualize the freedom that comes next—more peace, more strength, more joy. Write one word that represents what you're inviting in.

Final Word

Releasing doesn't erase your story—it reclaims your power. You are not defined by what you carry. You are defined by your willingness to lay it down and keep walking.

The Inner Circle Club

**You've just stepped through something powerful.
Now it's time to speak on it and allow your "NET" Work!**

This is your space to connect, reflect, and build community with other readers.

CHAPTER 2: The Cost of Carrying It All

- What's one invisible weight you've been carrying for too long?

- Who or what helps you put it down and breathe again?

- How do you honor your past without letting it define your present?

Pause. Breathe. Look within. Use this space to unpack the day—what moved you, challenged you, or taught you. Every moment holds meaning.

Daily Reflection Journal

Date _____ / _____ / _____

Mood Tracker

Choose a face   😐 🙂 😌 😍 😀 😟

Add a description _____

_____

_____

Highlights of the day

01	_____
02	_____
03	_____
04	_____
05	_____
06	_____
07	_____

Gratitude List ☆☆

_____

_____

_____

_____

_____

_____

What I learned today

_____

_____

_____

_____

Goals for tomorrow

_____

_____

_____

CHAPTER 3:
HEALING IN REAL TIME

Opening Reflection

Life doesn't always break you all at once. Sometimes, it cracks you in places you don't even notice until one day, everything shatters. This chapter isn't told in perfect order — because real life rarely follows a straight line.

One moment there was a hard collision with truth about my health and my future. Another was a quiet collapse inside the family I had worked so hard to build.

Both were breaking points.
Both were turning points.
Both changed me forever.

This is the story of how a conversation, a crash, a cup left untouched, and a paper slid across a restaurant table all became the crossroads that demanded: *Will you stay broken, or will you start becoming?*

Each moment, whether unexpected or painful, forced me to confront who I had become and who I still had the chance to be.

When Rock Bottom Becomes the Foundation

A Day When I Was Challenged to Think Differently

I remember the moment vividly—my father sitting in his usual spot, a chair just inside my bedroom doorway, the way he always did when we had one of our long talks. But this time was different.

He looked at me with a quiet intensity, not with anger or disappointment, but with something deeper—concern, love, and an undeniable truth he needed me to hear.

Then he asked the question that would change my life:

> *"Do you want your son to take care of you like you are taking care of us?"*

It landed like a punch to the gut.

I was in the throes of caring for both of my parents. Their medical needs had become my daily responsibility, and I was balancing work, family, and my own declining health, and if I'm being honest, I wasn't balancing much of anything. I was drowning.

At first, I wanted to be defensive. I wanted to say, "What do you mean? I've got this handled." But I didn't. Because deep down, I knew the truth.

I was at my heaviest weight. I was ignoring every warning sign my body gave me. And my drinking? I was convincing myself that it was just a way to relax, a social thing, nothing serious.

But my father's words exposed a reality I couldn't ignore:
If I didn't change, my son would be forced to care for me long before he should have to.
That wasn't fair to him.
That wasn't the legacy I wanted to leave.
That was the start of the moment.
That was the night I lay in bed and started questioning everything—my habits, my choices, my health, my future.
That was the beginning of a new journey.

But here's the thing about wake-up calls: sometimes one isn't enough. Even after that conversation with my father, even after the tears and the reflection, I didn't change overnight. I wish I could say I immediately got it together—but healing doesn't always happen in a straight line. Sometimes, even after being warned, we still crash.

Sometimes, the silence catches up to you louder than the sirens ever could.

And so, sometime after that pivotal talk, I found myself back at another crossroads, this time on a street called Lee Road, under flashing lights, facing the consequences I had spent too long trying to outrun.

But old habits die hard, and as I said earlier, growth doesn't follow a straight line. Just when I thought I had reached my bottom, life reminded me I had to fall further.

The Right to Remain Silent

May 12, 2016, started like any ordinary day—but it ended with a memory I'll never forget.

After work, I went out with a few HBCU alumni and colleagues; Lester, Heather and Carlie. We were scouting a venue for a potential alumni gathering. You know, somewhere casual with good food, good vibes. Wings, fries, and drinks were part of the plan. Actually, more than a few drinks – I had three top-shelf Long Islands Iced Teas. If you know, you know. That's not "light" sipping.

As the evening wound down, it was still bright outside, a typical spring afternoon. We were about to leave when a familiar voice called out:

"Brown, come through, have a drink with me!"

Against better judgment, and already feeling myself, I sat back down and enjoyed a few more Long Islands. I had no business doing it. None. Upon leaving the venue, I tried something I had done before when I knew I wasn't in the best shape to drive, by calling someone to stay on the phone with me. Listen, if you ever received a random phone call from me and I start off with, "Dude, I'm done," it means talk to me as I drive home. I thought that if I stayed talking, maybe I could stay alert. But this time, nobody picked up. So, I did the worst thing I could: I convinced myself I was fine.

I was less than ten minutes from home, driving down Lee Road in Shaker Heights, when it happened. Then it happened. A swerve. A dip. A sudden stop in the middle of the road. And then—the cherries and berries of police lights were behind me. Three squad cars. I froze.

In that moment, I wasn't just a man who had too much to drink. I was a Black man in 2016, living in a time when a simple traffic stop could feel like a life-or-death gamble. Remember,

➢ **Trayvon Martin** was just a teenager walking home with a bag of Skittles when his life was cut short.

➢ **Michael Brown** was a young man whose final moments in Ferguson sparked a national outcry.

- ➢ **Tamir Rice** was a 12-year-old boy playing in a Cleveland park, gunned down within seconds of police arriving.
- ➢ **Freddie Gray** took his final ride in the back of a police van, never making it home.

Each name wasn't just a headline. It was a warning. A prayer. A reminder that any misstep, any misunderstanding, any misinterpretation could cost me everything.

Fear swallowed me whole.

They cuffed me using two sets of handcuffs because of my size at the time and put me in the squad car. I wasn't even officially charged yet, and my whole life felt like it had collapsed.

I spent that night in jail. Didn't eat. I didn't use the bathroom. Hell, I didn't have my CPAP machine, so even breathing was a battle, so that meant that I didn't sleep.

At one point through my drunkenness, I spotted a guy in the cell that looked familiar. Come to find out, he was someone I once taught looking so lost and broken that moment nearly undid me. I don't even think he recognized me. Maybe that was the worst part: seeing reflections of brokenness, both his and mine, staring back at me.

When it came time to make that one phone call, I knew only two numbers by memory: my son's and my ex-wife's. So, with all the humiliation a man could muster, **I called my ex. And she answered.** After a few choice words, she was able to make some phone calls so that I could post bail. Another painful lesson wrapped in unexpected grace.

The next morning, my dad and son picked me up from the jail. Before heading home, we had to stop at the impound lot to retrieve my car. Talk about a ride that was so quiet it felt painfully deafening.

And yet, somehow, that afternoon, I still showed up at the historic Karamu House for a matinee performance. Students from the high school I worked at were in the audience, waiting to see their Dean of Students perform.

I made it through the afternoon show – foggy, ashamed, barely standing – but I couldn't make it through the evening performance. Thank God for understudies. I was broken in ways that even the stage lights, make-up and costumes couldn't hide.

The court dates came next. The mandatory AA meetings. The probation check-ins. The DUI sobriety classes.

And still...

At that point, deep down, I still didn't believe I had a drinking problem.

Not yet.

Keep walking with me. The story isn't over.

That night behind bars should have been my rock bottom. It should have been the wake-up call. But the truth is, change doesn't always come in the crashing moments. We often cling to denial until the weight becomes unbearable. My fight for sobriety didn't start overnight. It was slow unraveling, a battle between the lies I told myself and the truth that I refused to stay silent.

Jail was a wake-up call, but not loud enough to drown out my denial. I kept telling myself I was fine, even as the truth kept surfacing.

The Hard Truth Facing Alcoholism

After that humiliating night—the flashing lights, the cuffs, the jail cell, the uncomfortable ride home—you would think I would have gotten the message. You would think that embarrassment alone would have been enough to force a change.

Before I stopped drinking, my routine was simple:
Work. Eat. Drink. Repeat.

On an average night, I could easily down 32 ounces of vodka or tequila—sometimes more. According to the National Institute on Alcohol Abuse and Alcoholism, men are far more likely to binge drink and less likely to seek help. I was living that truth—using alcohol to numb what I wasn't ready to confront. Some nights, I'd sit alone, convincing myself it was just how I relaxed. Other nights, I'd be out with friends, running up bar tabs that made no sense.

Either way, I told myself the same lie: I'm still in control.
But the truth? I wasn't.
Even after:

- the flashing police lights on Lee Road...
- the cold metal of handcuffs...
- sitting in a jail cell...
- seeing one of my former students locked up beside me...

I still wasn't fully convinced.

Hi, my name is Anthony Brown, and I'm an alcoholic. I went through the motions because the court required it: AA meetings, a weekend sobriety course, monthly probation check-ins. Even after being in a jail cell wondering how my life had taken such a turn. I still wasn't convinced I had a problem.

I'd show up to the meetings just long enough to get my paperwork signed. I'd nod, pretend to listen, and leave the moment it was over. And more often than not, I'd go next door to the bar-b-que spot and pick me up a special (or two) then head straight to the liquor store afterward. In my mind, I wasn't drinking and driving. That's how deep my denial was. I wasn't ready to change because I didn't believe change was necessary yet.

Then came a house party of some HBCU alumni at a friend's house in Akron, Ohio. I told myself I'd be responsible this time. I even took a nap before leaving, thinking that would somehow "reset" my system and make it safe to drive. But the truth was, my system was already poisoned by alcohol, by arrogance, by the lie I kept telling myself that I could handle it.

And here's the thing:

> My body, my mind, my spirit – they were all still broken.
>
> Broken from years of pain.
>
> Broken from not loving myself.
>
> Broken from not believing I could be a true man of God.
>
> Broken from thinking I would never be a good father.

I was hurt. I was devastated. I was over it.

Then, on that rainy drive home late at night, I hit a rough patch—both in my life and on the road. Allegedly, I was driving a little too fast while entering the freeway on an on-ramp. I must have hit a slick spot, lost control of the car, and slammed into the concrete wall.

Yet, by the grace of God, the airbags never deployed, and somehow, I walked away physically unharmed. Evidently, I must have knocked myself sober, because by the time the police arrived, I was no longer behind the wheel—I was sitting on the side of the road, soaked from the rain, disgusted with myself, and numb to the weight of it all.

This encounter went differently than the last. The bad weather worked in my favor. The officers believed the out-of-control vehicle story and, rather than charging me with a DUI, they issued a citation and arranged for the car to be towed. Since I was out of their jurisdiction, they dropped me off at a nearby gas station. I called for an Uber and rode home in silence, soaking wet in more ways than one.

The next morning, reality hit even harder. I got a ride to the impound lot in Akron, where I saw the full extent of the damage under the harsh morning light. The car was totaled—completely done. And once again, my bank account didn't walk away unscathed. Court costs. Insurance hikes. A wrecked vehicle. Another mountain of consequences adding to the weight I was already carrying.

And still, I hadn't stopped. Not yet anyway. As the old folks would say, "a hard head..." well you know the rest. But sometimes, even when the wreckage piles up around you, it takes a quiet moment, not a crash, for real surrender to finally take root.

I had crashed more than my car. I had crashed into myself. And yet, the shift didn't come from flashing lights or courtrooms. It came in the quiet, when no one else was watching. It wasn't until a quiet flight home from attending a UNCF conference in Atlanta that everything finally shifted.

Thirty Thousand Feet to Freedom

The conference that weekend had been everything my spirit needed. From every session, every conversation; it wasn't just about alumni business or university pride. It was about legacy, leadership, and life. I had grown up in this organization, attending my first conference as a wide-eyed college student. Now, years later, I was the one pouring back into the students and young alumni following behind me.

One moment in particular still plays in my mind like a slow-motion highlight reel. During one of the afternoon workshop breaks, probably Thursday, Dr. Walter Dogan, a respected Morehouse College graduate and longtime mentor in the organization, pulled me aside. Dr. Dogan had watched me grow up over the years not just as a professional, but as a man. And in his quiet, fatherly way, he dropped a seed into my spirit and asked,

"Have you ever thought about running for national president?"

I laughed it off at first. The thought had crossed my mind, sure, but to hear him speak it aloud made it feel real. Serious. Heavy.

He smiled, the kind of smile a father gives when he's about to give advice with love.

"People are watching you, Anthony. Even when you think they aren't. They're watching. How you carry yourself matters."

Those words hit differently. It was like hearing my own father's voice echo through him—reminding me of the very talk we had back home when he asked,

"Do you want your son to take care of you the way you're taking care of us?"

The message was clear: Leadership wasn't just about who you are in the spotlight. It is about who you are when nobody is clapping. And it wasn't about being perfect it was about leaving a path worth following. I had a decision to make: Would I leave a trail of excuses and self-destruction, or a legacy of resilience and growth?

When Sunday arrived, I boarded my Southwest flight home to Cleveland with all of that swirling in my heart—gratitude for the conference, a deep sense of pride for the young people I had mentored, and a heavy reflection on the type of man I was still becoming. As I settled into my seat, muscle memory kicked in. Like clockwork, I reached for the drink voucher tucked in my pocket to partake in the free drink that I always looked forward to after a long conference.

I ordered a tequila sunrise. It arrived perfectly mixed—the orange juice settling at the bottom, the tequila layered through the ice, the condensation glistening on the cup like sweat. It looked so inviting, so familiar. One of my favorite travel rituals.

But as I stared at the drink, something shifted.

Pride from the weekend.

The weight of Dr. Dogan's words.

The image of my father.

The thought of my son.

All of it collided in my spirit at 30,000 feet in the air.

There I was miles and miles above the earth, suspended between two worlds—the man I had been, and the man I was being called to become. Then I took a sip... and for the first time, it didn't taste right. It tasted like regret. Like wasted potential. Like shame. And then, somewhere between the clouds and the heavens, the sky and the earth below, from the hum of the engines and the prayers of the righteous, I whispered two words to myself, to God, to the universe:

> **"I quit."**

Not with anger. Not with fear. With peace. With finality.

And for the first time in years, I didn't *want* it.

I didn't *need* it.

I didn't *miss* it.

I didn't *take* another sip.

I didn't *second-guess* it.

> *"My grace is sufficient for you, for my power is made perfect*

in weakness." — **2 Corinthians 12:9**

That day in the sky, I didn't find willpower. I found grace. His strength showed up when mine ran out.

I just sat there and watched that cup sweat and settle. By the time the plane landed, the drink was still full. Untouched. Unbothered. Seemingly flat from the melted ice. Once upon a time, I would have joked that leaving a drink behind was alcohol abuse.

But this time? I didn't care.
This time, it was over.

February 18, 2018, became my new beginning.
My sobriety date.
My covenant with myself to walk a different road.

I didn't know exactly what the road ahead would look like. I just knew I was ready to walk it sober, free, and finally awake. But the consequences of my choices didn't just have an impact on my health or my freedom. They rippled into the very heart of my family. It was poor decisions like this that would cost me one of the greatest relationships I ever had.

Final Thought: A Legacy of Change

My father's question wasn't about guilt. It was about awareness. It was a call to evaluate the choices I was making and their impact on my future.

In the end, the choices we make today ripple out into the lives of those we love.

So, take a moment to reflect:
What habits are you passing down—intentionally or unintentionally?

_____

_____

_____

Are you building a legacy of strength, or one of struggle?

_____

_____

_____

If your child had to follow in your footsteps, would you be proud of where they lead?

_____

_____

_____

Change starts with awareness. Legacy is built on action.

Building a Family Before the Break

From College Sweethearts to Marriage

My ex-wife and I were more than just college sweethearts; we were two people who, from the very beginning, decided to navigate life together. From the day we met in freshman year, we didn't have all the answers, but we had each other. And that was enough to get us through. We shared our dreams, our struggles, our triumphs, and our setbacks.

Our love was built on mutual respect and the desire to make things work, no matter what life handed our way. In those early years of marriage, it felt like nothing could break us. We were young, hopeful, and full of plans. We sang in the choir together, took trips to visit her family in Florida, and spent countless hours just getting to know each other.

I remember the excitement of starting life together, working hard, supporting each other's ambitions, and building a home that was full of love, even when we didn't have much. In those first years of marriage, I never questioned the strength of our bond. We were partners, and everything we did was in pursuit of a shared vision.

The Birth of Our Son: A New Beginning

Then came the moment that changed everything: the birth of our son. I had never known love in that way before. Watching him enter the world, and knowing that I was part of his creation, filled me with a sense of purpose I hadn't experienced before.

Becoming a father made me question everything. I had to shift my focus from just being a husband to being a father, a protector, a provider, and a teacher. I remember the first diaper change, the first time I held him in my arms, and I knew that my life had changed forever. I couldn't stop looking at him and wondering, "How am I going to do this?"

In the beginning, I didn't know what I was doing, but the love I felt for him made me all in. It wasn't just about being a good husband anymore, it was about being a good father. And that role, I learned quickly, was not easy. I had to dig deep within myself to rise to the occasion, even when I didn't feel equipped. But parenting doesn't exist in a vacuum, it transforms everything around it, including the very foundation of your relationship.

The Transition: From Couple-hood to Parenthood

Parenthood was a beautiful but challenging transition for both of us. There were sleepless nights, moments of doubt, and a struggle to balance our new roles. At first, I was excited, but then the weight of responsibility hit me. I couldn't just be a husband anymore, I had to be a father, and that came with its own set of challenges.

It was hard. It was tiring. But it was also the most rewarding experience of my life. My love for my son pushed me to become better, to be better. Even in those moments when I doubted myself, I knew I had to keep moving forward, for him. And despite the challenges, there was a deep connection that grew stronger every day. But as our son grew and life became more complex, the bond between us quietly began to shift.

And as the seasons changed, so did we. Not in a single moment, but in slow, silent ways that neither of us had the words to name.

The Shift in Our Relationship

But the reality of marriage and family life wasn't as perfect as we had imagined. We rode in the same car to church on Sunday mornings. We slept in the same bed at night. We said good morning. We said good night. But in between those hours? We barely spoke. I thought the love we had would always be enough to keep us going. But love alone wasn't holding us together anymore. Somewhere along the way, what started as a deeply rooted connection began to fade—slowly, almost silently. Not from a single argument or betrayal, but from the weight of everything life threw at us.

It was the kind of distance that creeps in over time. You don't always see it happening, you just wake up one day and realize the intimacy is gone. We were living under the same roof, but it felt like we were in separate worlds. There were bills, a baby, work, deadlines, church obligations, and never enough time to just... be with each other.

The rhythm that once bonded us – the inside jokes, the late-night talks, the spontaneous road trips – was now replaced with routine, responsibility, and resignation. It wasn't a loud breakup. It was a quiet unraveling. The kind where everything looks intact from the outside, but on the inside—it's dust and distance. The intimacy faded slowly. It wasn't just physical, it was spiritual and emotional, too. The laughter turned into reminders. The late-night talks disappeared into silence.

Don't get me wrong, I still loved her. But I'm not sure I was in love with her anymore. There's a difference. Love was still present, but the spark had dimmed. It wasn't about infidelity or betrayal. It was about how the demands of life began to outpace the intentionality of connection.

I found myself immersed in my work and distracted from my family. On paper, I was doing everything right. I was providing. I was present at events. I financially supported the birthdays and holidays. But emotionally? I was gone.

We were co-existing, not co-creating. And that's when I knew: even if love was still in the room, it wasn't holding us together anymore.

I remember the sting of her voice one evening when she said,

> *"It's funny how you have a degree in mass communication and can talk to everyone but me."*

That line landed like a punch to the chest. And she was right, and it cut deep. Because it was true. Somehow, I had forgotten how to talk to the one person I used to share everything with. I could lead meetings, inspire rooms, host a show, but at home, I was silent. I shut down and was guarded.

And the truth is, I didn't want to address it. I knew something was broken, but I didn't know how to fix it—or if I even had the energy to try. Instead, I kept showing up in the expected ways—working, parenting, paying bills—but emotionally, I had checked out. I had become the very thing I swore I wouldn't: a man who hides behind his roles instead of leaning into his relationship. She kept showing up and I didn't.

And here's the thing, she was still showing up. Through every life transition I experienced, like when I went back to grad school, when I left my tenured teaching job after 12 years, when I chased opportunities in television, through deaths in the family, during my personal crises, she stayed. When I traveled for work and left her with our child, she never complained, not that I know of. But when she wanted to pursue something for herself? Either I wasn't there… or I found a way to make it about me.

Looking back now, I realize she was willing to ride with me until the wheels fell off. But I never matched that level of commitment—not emotionally. And if I did, I sure as hell didn't show it.

Living Up to Expectations

Throughout all of this, I found myself caught between three versions of what it meant to be a man: what I believed, what society expected, and what she needed.

I didn't question my identity as a man in the physical sense—but the emotional weight of manhood, of how it's defined and performed, became a constant struggle. What did it really mean to be a good man? A real man? A Black man? The answers shifted depending on who you asked.

Society told me a man was stoic. A provider. The strong, silent type. Someone who didn't cry, didn't complain, didn't ask for help. However, I was ready for a quick one-liner, comeback, or quip. I saw it on TV growing up—James Evans, Fred Sanford, Cliff Huxtable, George Jefferson. They all seemed to solve everything in 22 minutes. But my problems and my life weren't a sitcom. It didn't come with commercial breaks, a live studio audience, or a laugh track. There was no quick resolution, no feel-good moment at the end of each episode. Just long days of pretending everything was fine. If anything, my life felt like an episode that never ended. I was stuck in a script that no one taught me how to flip to the next scene.

She, on the other hand, needed a man who was consistent. Emotionally present. Spiritually grounded. A communicator. Someone who could lead with love, not just provision. And the truth is—she had every right to want that. She showed up for me in ways that I couldn't always return. I recall her stepfather, John, had been a steady presence in her life. Maybe that baseline, whether conscious or not, might've shaped how she measured manhood. And eventually, I just didn't measure up.

And then there was me. I didn't like sports. I wasn't a flirt. I didn't change oil, cut grass, or fix things. That wasn't me.

What did I love? Musicals. Art museums. Choir rehearsals. Long walks through the mall. Comic Books. Deep conversations. Worship nights at church. But around other men, especially my male cousins, I always felt out of place. Like my brand of manhood wasn't "man enough."

So, for a long time I struggled with the understanding and comprehension of what a man was. From the physical perspective, which was obvious. But the emotional weight? The spiritual burden? I was lost.

I think one of the biggest influences on my idea of manhood weren't people around me, the TV fathers, or any male relatives; it was my own father who once told me,

"Son, never argue with a woman. Just be quiet, and it'll pass."
That was his version of masculinity. To be detached, avoidant, and dismissive. I inherited that silence and brought it into my marriage, hoping disagreements would just disappear if I said nothing. But silence only made the gap between us wider. It took years for me to realize that I wasn't just repeating my father's behavior, I was reacting to a silence I never learned to break.

The performance of masculinity, trying to be what everyone else expected, was also a struggle within itself. This left me disconnected from myself. I wasn't fully authentic. And trying to support that illusion wore me down. I wasn't leading with honesty, vulnerability, or self-awareness. I was just surviving.

Research confirms that this type of role strain, especially for men navigating multiple and conflicting gender expectations can lead to anxiety, emotional withdrawal, and relationship breakdowns (Mahalik et al., 2003).

In the process, I lost my joy. I lost the connection. And worst of all, I started to lose myself. And then, in a moment that seemed ordinary on the surface, the illusion finally broke.

May I Have Some More Cheddar Biscuits

And then came the moment that shattered everything. We went out for dinner one evening, to Red Lobster, a place that had been one of our favorites. We were having a typical night out, or so I thought. We were actually laughing, chatting, and enjoying each other's company—until she slid the divorce papers across the table.

It was a moment of pure devastation. My world came to a screeching halt. All the questions I had about our relationship, our family, and my future came crashing down on me in that instant. I hadn't seen it coming, not like this.

I wanted to fix it. I wanted to make it all go away, to buy her something or say the right thing to make everything right again. But there was nothing I could do. The decision had already been made.

I was left there, at the table, with this undeniable lump on my throat trying to process what had just happened. The person I had spent so many years with, the one I had loved and shared my life with — was now telling me that it was over. And with tears rolling down my face, I couldn't do a damn thing to change it.

I can't say I didn't see it coming, but I hadn't fully realized how much my personal identity and self-worth were wrapped up in our relationship. As the news sank in, I began to feel a deep sense of personal failure. In the space of a few minutes, everything I thought

I knew about myself, about what I was capable of and who I was in relation to my family was thrown into question. What came next was more than the end of a marriage, it was the unraveling of the man I thought I was.

Emotional Toll and the Struggle with Identity

My reaction? I tried to fix it. I wondered what I could buy her, what I could say, how I could make this pain go away. But there was no quick fix. The decision had been made, and in a moment of clarity, I realized this wasn't about fixing the situation. It was about navigating the new reality. I had to let go.

> *"...to bestow on them a crown of beauty instead of ashes, the oil of joy instead of mourning..."* — **Isaiah 61:3**

Even in ashes, God was preparing beauty. Even through mourning, joy would come.

We parted ways amicably, but the emotional scars lingered. She got the dog—I didn't want the dog anyway—and I got the house and our son. We shared custody, but his primary residence became with me. That was a blessing, during it all, but it didn't make things easy. Maintaining a house alone was harder than I thought. And raising a teenager? That wasn't a walk in the park either.

I mean, this was no victory lap. It was survival mode. The mortgage, the meals, the moods, the homework, the silence. Some nights I just sat on the edge of the bed, asking myself, how did we get here?

After the divorce, I felt like a shadow of the man I once was. My self-worth—so deeply rooted in being a provider, a protector, and a partner—crumbled. I had built my identity on the image of being the "good man." But without the marriage, the house full of laughter, the shared holidays, and the shared dreams… who was I?

There were days when I couldn't bring myself to leave the house. I was embarrassed to be seen in public. Not because of what people may say, but because of what they might think. The questions ran wild in my head: Am I broken? Was I not enough? Is this what failure looks like?

The weight of unmet expectations – hers, society's, my own – began to suffocate me. I didn't want to talk about it, so I didn't. I just shut down. That silence became my own prison. If you continue to live to others' expectations, you will find yourself trapped in an endless cycle of perpetual turmoil. And that cycle? It comes with consequences.

I'm not even going to hold you – it was during this time that my struggle with alcohol really started to show its ugly head. The pressure of holding everything together; the house, the bills, being present for my son, showing up to work like I had it all figured out, was overwhelming. And when the silence got too loud, or the guilt crept in late at night, I drank. Not socially. Not casually. But to cope. I used it to numb the guilt, to quiet the questions, to take the edge off the silence that hung in the house after my son went to bed. The thing about pain is that it doesn't always scream—it creeps in, subtle and slick, until you don't even recognize yourself anymore.

The pressure to be strong, to keep moving, to make it all look easy wore me down. I'd show up for work with a smile, check the homework, cook dinner, and lay down at night... but the silence was deafening. The grief, the guilt, the questions about who I was and whether I was enough didn't go away. So, I drank. Not for fun. Not to celebrate. But to numb the pain. What started as a glass here and there turned into a habit I couldn't control. I wasn't drinking because I didn't care—I was drinking because I cared too much and didn't know what to do with all that pain. That season of my life became a blur of over-functioning in public and unraveling in private. And I didn't want to admit it, but I was drowning. Quietly.

I didn't realize it at the time, but I was withdrawing emotionally from everyone who mattered. I wasn't just shutting down, I was done. Avoidance is a better word. I was performing a version of healing I hadn't actually earned, yet. And when you sit in silence long enough, anxiety creeps in. Not the loud, panicked kind. But the quiet kind. The kind that wraps around your neck like a scarf in the summer, suffocating you with a smile.

And yes, I know about addiction, too. Not always the kind you think. Sometimes it's addiction to work. To validation. To busyness. To being needed. Sometimes it's just an addiction to escape anything to avoid sitting in the truth of your brokenness.

I had always prided myself on being a provider, a protector, a loving partner. Now, I was unsure of who I was in the world. I questioned my worth. I struggled to reconcile the man I had been with the man I was now becoming.

Studies show that many men, especially Black men, experience intense psychological strain when trying to balance traditional masculine expectations with emotional authenticity. That tension often leads to increased levels of depression, substance use, and relational breakdown (Hammond, 2012).

I would often find myself struggling to get through the holiday season, wishing I could just fast-forward from Thanksgiving straight into January. The depression, guilt, and sorrow were overwhelming, and there were days when all I could do was lay in bed and try to numb the pain. And when I couldn't numb it with distractions or fake smiles, I just avoided it altogether. I shut down, just like I had learned from my father, hoping if I said nothing, it would all eventually pass. But silence doesn't heal anything. It only deepens the wound.

This was the emotional cost of living up to everyone else's

expectations but my own. I had internalized the idea that my job was to show up, provide, protect, and pretend. But inside? I was unraveling.

The most honest thing I can offer in this moment is this: Learn to love yourself without performing for anyone else's approval. Choose the life that brings you peace—the work that sustains you, the joy that feeds your soul, the path that aligns with who you truly are. Because the moment you start living by someone else's script for manhood, family, or success, you risk losing yourself. And that loss doesn't come all at once—it shows up quietly, as burnout, as silence, as a version of you that no longer feels like home.

That kind of disconnection isn't just inconvenient—it's dangerous. It chips away at your voice, your relationships, and your sense of self. Left unchecked, it breeds silence, isolation, and sometimes addiction. I've lived it. I've worn the mask, played the role, and nearly lost myself in the process.

But even in the quiet unraveling, a flicker of hope remained. I just had to be honest enough to stop pretending—and brave enough to begin again. Because healing rarely starts with perfection. Sometimes, it begins with a quiet yes to something different. Something true.

A Christmas Revelation: The Power of Family

It wasn't until 2024 that things started to change. I decided to get out of my self-imposed isolation and spend Thanksgiving with my aunt and cousins in Atlanta. For Christmas, my oldest cousin's daughter invited me to her house for the first time. At first, I didn't want to go. I wasn't ready to engage. But my family wouldn't take no for an answer.

They were determined to not let me celebrate the holiday alone. Baby girl called me repeatedly and insisted that I would attend brunch. And so, after a long hesitation, I arrived shortly after 3:00 PM, and they hadn't even started cooking. The entire household waited for me.

They welcomed me in, making sure I felt like I was part of a family again. It wasn't just about the food, it was about familial love, the sense of community, the support. The importance of family didn't hit me until that moment. They had created a space for me, refusing to let me spend Christmas by myself, and for the first time in years, I felt seen, loved, and cared for.

That Christmas, I wasn't just battling the weight of the past. I was beginning to create new memories with the people who mattered most. While I wasn't ready to put up a Christmas tree or fully embrace the holiday spirit in my home, I knew I had my family. And that, at that moment, was enough. That season didn't magically erase the pain, but it reminded me that I wasn't alone, and that grace could show up through community, even after the loss.

There Is A. B.etter Way

But time and intention can turn even heartbreak into healing. Divorce doesn't always mean destruction. Sometimes, it's just the final chapter in one book so you can begin another with a clearer pen. That's what it became for Latasha and me.

We learned how to coexist, how to raise a child in love even after the romance faded. We learned how to partner in ways that didn't require matching last names. We learned how to create something meaningful out of everything we thought we lost.

Today, we are not just co-parents, we're collaborators. We built something together that neither of us could've done alone:

A. B.etter Way Productions, LLC.

Now look, if I had my way, I would've called the company, Anthony Brown's Way, but of course, she wasn't feeling that. Which is probably why she's my ex-wife (well that's how I tell the story). So, we compromised. And what we settled on was something even better: a name that reminded us that no matter the challenge, the detour, or the setback – there's always A. B.etter Way forward.

Together, we created a company designed to support students, families, and emerging leaders, especially those attending or aspiring to attend HBCUs. Our mission is to offer: One-on-One Mentoring, College and Career Prep, Professional Development, Life Coaching, Parent/Student Workshops, and Community Service. It's not just a business. It's a legacy.

We didn't plan for this path. But even in the end, we created something that still lives on and maybe that's what love really looks like when it matures. Not always romantic. But purposeful. Impactful. Rooted in growth.

When she remarried years after our divorce, I was there at her invitation and George's. Yes, her husband personally reached out and welcomed me to the celebration. That meant something. And truth be told, we all get along great. We support each other, we show up for our son, and we move forward with mutual respect. I like to joke that I went to the wedding just to get my last name back. But honestly? In many professional spaces, she still uses it.

Her using my last name is not the concern, because what we built – our son, our bond, our business – still carries the imprint of something real. We're not a perfect story. But we are a powerful story.

Final Thought: Embracing the Break & Building a New Self

Divorce is never easy, but it's also a chance for reinvention and growth. It's an opportunity to shed the weight of unmet expectations and begin to redefine who you are. Letting go of a marriage, no matter the circumstances, is difficult, but it's not the end of your story.

What parts of your identity are tied to relationships that no longer serve you?

_____

_____

_____

How can you redefine yourself after a significant life change?

_____

_____

_____

What steps can you take today to start building a healthier, more authentic version of yourself?

_____

_____

_____

Change is never easy, but it's always an opportunity to gain experience. The future is waiting for you to step into it, unburdened by the weight of yesterday. Take the lessons, let go of the baggage, and create the life you're meant to lead.

Inspire Me Moment: Still Winning or Learning

Every pivotal moment in life teaches us something—if we're willing to listen. Whether in success or setbacks, we are constantly evolving, learning, and growing. The key is understanding that every challenge is an opportunity. As you reflect on your own path, remember you're either winning or learning.

"My life is full of mistakes; they're like pebbles and make a good road."
Beatrice Wood

Reflection:
Mistakes are a part of life. But how often do we dwell on them longer than necessary, forgetting that others have already moved on? The real question isn't about the mistake itself; it's about how you recover and reshape the narrative into something positive.

Setbacks are inevitable—but what if you expected them, prepared for them, and even embraced them? Growth isn't about avoiding failure; it's about recognizing that every misstep, challenge, and unexpected turn is a steppingstone to something greater. Every lesson is shaping you into the person you're meant to be.

Final Thought:
You're either winning or learning, there is no losing, only opportunities to grow. Embrace the journey, own your lessons, and keep building the road ahead.

Live Out Loud Challenge:
Still Winning or Learning

Every setback holds a lesson. This challenge invites you to reframe failure—not as a defeat, but as a doorway to deeper growth, resilience, and renewal.

Connect

Reach out to someone you admire, someone who has turned failure into a foundation. Ask: *"What perspective helped you transform your setback into strength—and how do you keep moving forward?"*

Reflect

Revisit a past mistake, disappointment, or missed opportunity. Journal or talk with a trusted friend, mentor, or peer. Ask yourself: *"What wisdom did I gain from this experience that my younger self wouldn't have understood?"*

Support

Encourage someone who may be struggling right now. Remind them: *"Failure isn't the opposite of success, it's a critical part of the journey. Every stumble teaches you how to soar."*

Wellness Check-In
The Moment Everything Changed

Purpose: Transformation often begins in chaos or discomfort. This check-in helps you name the shift, reflect on the lessons, and step forward with intention.

Today I will stop...

Carrying fear from what changed yesterday. I no longer allow the unexpected to define my future.

Today I will start...

Reclaiming my story with confidence. I will own my growth even when it starts to be in pain.

This truth will anchor me...

"I trust that every change in my life is leading me toward purpose and growth."

This one action will move me forward...

I will take one bold step that aligns with the person I'm becoming. Whether it's reaching out for support, setting a boundary, or finally choosing myself—I move forward today.

The Inner Circle Club

You've just stepped through something powerful.
Now it's time to speak on it and allow your "NET" Work!

This is your space to connect, reflect, and build community with other readers.

CHAPTER 3: *Healing in Real Time*

- What does it mean to heal *in real time* look like for you right now?

- Can you name a breaking point that became a turning point?

- How do you hold space for your pain without being consumed by it?

CHAPTER 4:
MY NAME IS VICTORY

Opening Reflection

There are nights when life doesn't just shake you, it breaks you wide open.

Not in stages. Not in pieces.

But in a wave so fierce, it drags you under before you even realize you're drowning.

This chapter begins on one of those nights.

A migraine became a moment.

A song of praise became a cry for help.

A hospital gown replaced my Sunday best.

And a word I had only whispered in prayer, cancer was suddenly being spoken over my name.

But even in that chaos, something Holy was happening.

In the space between diagnosis and deliverance, I came face-to-face with fear, faith, and the fight to live again.

I didn't just confront my health; I confronted the weight I had been carrying in silence. The shame, the guilt, the need to be strong for everyone but myself.

This is not just the story of a scan or a second opinion.

It's the story of what happens when the soul gets backed up.

When pressure meets purpose.

When a man finally decides he's tired of being full of pain, pride, trauma—and yes, even $#IT.

Because healing doesn't always begin with medicine.

Sometimes, it begins with surrender.

So, if you've ever felt stuck, suffocated, or scared to let go, lean in.

This chapter is for you.

It's the story of a midnight breakdown,

a third-day breakthrough,

and the sacred work of learning to live light again.

A Midnight Call

A Word I Never Wanted to Hear

Having taken care of both my parents through their health battles, I've met a lot of medical challenges. But there was one word that always struck fear in me—cancer. It seemed like it had a way of weaving itself into conversations, diagnoses, and lives. I had managed to move around blessed, untouched—until the day the word came too close.

When I first heard the word cancer associated with my name, I was in a state of confusion. I was heavily medicated and didn't really know what was happening. I was in a dreamlike state, barely able to process anything. The pain was so intense it felt like I was having an out-of-body experience.

Long before I found myself in that hospital bed, the signs were already there. They were subtle warnings my body had been whispering for years.

The Mystery of the Migraines

Years before I faced what would become one of my biggest health scares, I was dealing with unbearable migraines. The kind that stole my energy, disrupted my days, and made me question everything I was doing. We tried everything, adjusting my diet, eliminating scents, reducing light exposure—yet the migraines remained unpredictable and debilitating.

One doctor's visit changed everything. As he examined me, he started running tests, checking my reflexes, and then he shined that dreaded light into my eyes. I told him,

"You want to see a migraine happen? Watch this."

Sure enough, within moments, the light triggered an episode. My entire body shut down. I couldn't move. I passed out right there in the doctor's office.

When Worship Turns into a Wake-Up Call

A few weeks later, I was in church. That morning, I had been out the night before, still drinking, still carrying the weight of an unhealthy lifestyle. But I showed up, like I always did, standing with the praise team, singing:

"I just want to praise You forever and ever..."

We were having *high church*—hands raised, voices lifted. I had felt a little dizzy, but I figured it was just the effects of the night before. Then, out of nowhere, that migraine hit me like a storm. I got dizzy, my words slurred, and my body started shutting down again.

At first, the congregation thought I was just *deep in worship*. They cheered me on, saying, *"Let Him use you!"* They had no idea I was crying out for help. During the song, I even ad-libbed, saying something like *"God, take this pain away"*—but they thought I was speaking metaphorically. Then, I hit the floor. I blacked out.

The next thing I knew, I woke up in an ambulance. For a moment, I thought I had crossed over—I saw a figure in all white, surrounded by light, and I swore I was stepping into glory. It turns out, it was my wife at the time, dressed in white, riding with me to the hospital.

The Diagnosis That Was

I woke up in a hospital bed, my head pounding, my vision blurry. As I tried to make sense of where I was, I overheard doctors speaking in hushed voices. They were concerned about lesions spreading throughout my brain.

Mind you, I was heavily sedated, but what I thought I heard was:

> *"It looks like he may have brain cancer."*

The words that I feared, and the weight of those words settled deep. Brain cancer? Me? Was this how my story ended? The hours that followed were a blur of tests and prayers. I was still floating between sedation and confusion, unsure what was real and what was imagined.

Finding Out My Fate... on Facebook

Sometime in the midnight hour, after waves of tests and scans, I woke up. I did what most of us do, I reached for my phone. I scrolled through social media, only to see my name plastered all over with prayer requests.

"Lord, cover Deacon Brown!"

"Praying for healing over his body."

"Cancer will not win!"

I was detached from the moment as this was all surreal to me. I was reading those posts as if they weren't about me. I felt like I was reading about some other guy named Anthony, not realizing it was me.

I called a friend, Charles Cotton, to make sense of it all. He hit me with words that stopped me in my tracks:

"Anthony, before you knew what they said you had, you got up every morning. Now that you know—does that stop you from living?"

That hit like a ton of bricks.

He reminded me: Just because I knew the diagnosis didn't mean it had power over me. Faith wasn't just in my worship—it was in how I responded to the storm.

The Power of the Third Day

Sunday turned to Monday, Monday to Tuesday. Latasha asked for a second opinion before they made any drastic decisions.

They ran another round of tests. Then came the third day.

"Mr. & Mrs. Brown… what we thought we saw… we don't see anymore."

What they thought was cancer—was gone.

I couldn't help but think about another third day experience. The day when death was defeated, and life was restored. The same way Jesus rose with all power, I felt like I had been given a second chance.

The doctors showed me the scans—it was like night and day. On the left, my brain was covered in lesions. On the right, a nearly clear image. The diagnosis was gone, but the testimony remained.

It reminded me of how sometimes we must go through our own crucifixion moments. The pain, the fear, the darkness—feeling like all hope is lost. But just like Jesus got up, my third day came with a resurrection of my faith, my strength, and my belief in miracles.

Tears began to roll down my face. Just a few days before, they were ready to bust my head wide open. I sat there in disbelief. The test came back clean. They had no medical explanation. Just like that, I had my life back. My son had his father. My mother had her son. I had another chance.

It felt like a divine moment—like I had just lived out the truth in Psalm 30:5: *"Weeping may endure for a night, but joy comes in the morning"* (New International Version). I'd heard that verse all my life but now I have lived it. My darkest night became a doorway to a brighter dawn. That wasn't just a medical miracle. It was a spiritual reminder that God still moves mountains.

Now some kind of scar tissue still remains on my brainstem, just as the holes from the nails remained in His hands and feet. This serves as a reminder of suffering, but also a symbol of victory. A permanent mark of what I went through to get to the other side.

Victory on the Other Side

That experience became my testimony. The song I once sang from memory, I now sing from revelation:

> *I got evidence, I got confidence, I'm a conqueror, I know that I'll win…*
>
> *I know who I am, God wrote it in His plan for me. My name is Victory.*

I don't know who Jonathan Nelson had in mind when he wrote that song—but I know it was meant for me. The lyrics continued to say:

> *"He said that I've over come. I know I've already won. He wrote it my destiny. That my name is Victory."*

Sometimes, you must go through to get to. What they thought was the end of my story was just the setup for another testimony. And the story isn't over.

This chapter of my life could have ended with a dire diagnosis, but instead, it ends with destiny. I walked out of that hospital not just healed but transformed.

Final Thought: Living Beyond the Diagnosis

What storm have you been through that felt like the end, but was it really the beginning?

_____

_____

_____

_____

How are you choosing to live beyond the obstacles placed in front of you?

_____

_____

_____

_____

Are you letting fear write your story, or are you standing in faith?

_____

_____

_____

Faith isn't just about believing—it's about moving forward, even when the path is uncertain. Because on the other side of the storm—there's victory.

We're All Full of $#IT

The Truth We Carry, The Healing We Avoid

There's a saying you probably won't hear in a Sunday morning sermon or find wrapped in a pretty font on Instagram, but it might be the most honest truth I've lived:

> *We're all full of $#it (Sugar-Honey-Ice-Tea) – and we gotta get it out.*

And no, I'm not just talking about colon health – though trust me, that's a conversation we need to normalize too. I am talking about the emotional backup. The mental pressure. The spiritual congestion. The stuff we stack inside because we've been conditioned to "man up," stay silent, and keep pushing.

We walk around with stress packed behind our smiles, trauma tucked beneath our titles, and pain disguised as productivity. We don't talk about it until something breaks—or until our bodies start sounding alarms we can't ignore. And that's where this story begins.

A Night Meant for Men's Healing

It started as a simple idea. A night of brotherhood, healing, and care.

Together with the CMSD Men of Color Shaping Academics (MOCHA) Network and Profound Gentlemen Ohio, we hosted a men's health and wellness event at the University Hospitals Ahuja

Medical Center – Cutler Center for Men in Beachwood, Ohio. We called it "The Man Cave Recharging Station."

But this wasn't your average health fair.

We wanted something intentional, something that didn't feel like another after-work obligation. So, we flipped the script. This was about redefining self-care for Black and Brown men in education. This was about creating a space that felt familiar and restorative. We made it a vibe.

There were pool tables and card games. Laughter echoed over soft jazz and old-school R&B. Health trivia circled the room while barbers gave clean lineups in one corner and massage therapists eased tension in another. Fresh food, wine, good conversation, affirmations. When I tell you it all flowed, it flowed. We weren't just gathered; we were grounding ourselves in something sacred.

Men of color educators from the Cleveland Metropolitan School District, Shaker Heights, Euclid, Warrensville Heights, and nearby charter schools came together – not for training, not for compliance – but to breathe, to be seen, and to be whole.

We called it "Relax. Relate. Release."
And we meant every word.

- RELAX: We played spades, we sipped, we laughed like brothers on a front porch at sunset.

- RELATE: We swapped stories about the school year, the students who challenged us, the ones who inspired us. We got real about the burnout, the silent battles, the weight of always being "the strong one."

- RELEASE: We checked our vitals, had conversations with medical staff, got blood pressure readings, blood sugar levels, and even consulted about prostate health. Grooming services and professional headshots turned this event into something that not only healed but celebrated us.

I was proud to help organize it. But I knew I couldn't just be the guy handing out flyers or greeting guests at the door. I had to take part. So, I did. I signed up for a screening. I sat in the chair like everyone else. I wanted to show that taking care of yourself is not weakness, it's wisdom. But I didn't expect to become the poster child from the event.

The First Warning: High Blood Pressure

A few days later, the first test came back:

"Mr. Brown, your blood pressure's a little high."

What they found was that the "top number" in that blood pressure reading was reading a little high, but not nearly like it was in years past. Nothing dramatic, just elevated. I had been on mild medication before, so I figured they'd just bump up my dosage. No big deal, right? Compared to what I used to take in the heavier days, this was a breeze.

The Second Warning: A Family Legacy I Didn't Want

Then came another follow-up call.

> *"Mr. Brown, do you have a history of prostate cancer in your family?"*

Yes. My dad and his brother.

At the time of the event, I had already lost my father to prostate cancer. And only the Lord knew that seven years later I would lose my uncle too.

But I digress, several days later after the man cave event, I received a call from the clinic nurse. This wasn't just a routine follow-up. It was an alarm. My PSA numbers were climbing. The screening wasn't standard anymore, it was urgent.

Then came the nerve-wracking Magnetic Resonance Imaging (MRI) procedure. Let me tell you, being inside that tight and clicking tube felt like being trapped in the lower deck of the Titanic. Alarms.

Beeps. The howling metallic echoes. My anxiety was bubbling up—pressing against my chest just as hard as the fears racing through my mind.

The days leading up to that scan were a mess. I couldn't think straight. Sleep was scarce. My thoughts were spiraling:

> *What if? How bad is it? Am I next? Is this the same path my father walked?*

After all the tests, family history questions, screenings, and sleepless nights came the call.

The Third Warning: The Call That Made Me Pause

A few days after the scan, my phone rang. It was the nurse. She was friendly but she came with a lot of information. Maybe too much.

She started rattling off numbers, metrics, something about elevated PSA levels. She mentioned my family history. Said it "couldn't be ruled out." It felt like she was reading off a checklist—clinical, cautious, and covering every base. I tried to keep up, but the more she talked, the more I felt lost.

Finally, I had to stop her.

> *"Wait... are you saying I have cancer or not?"*

There was a pause. Then she said,

"No, you do not have cancer."

I exhaled like I had been underwater.

But just as I started to feel relief, she added:

> *"However, due to your elevated numbers and your family history, we strongly recommend annual prostate screenings, possibly sooner if any symptoms arise."*

That's when the weight of it all landed.

One in six Black men are diagnosed with prostate cancer in their lifetime. We're more than twice as likely to die from it compared to white men (Prostate Cancer Foundation, 2024).

That statistic stayed with me like a siren in my mind. Knowing both my father and uncle lost their lives to prostate cancer, that "spike" didn't feel small. It felt like a flare in the dark. A red flag waving right in my face.

The test was negative.
But the concern?
Still loud and clear.

I didn't receive a diagnosis that day.
But I did receive something just as powerful:
A warning.

A wake-up call.

Another chance.

And I knew—I had to listen.

The Gut Punch (Literally)

About a month later, I got another call.

> *"Mr. Brown, some of your levels from your last blood test look concerning. We want to check your colon."*

Now I'm tripping, tripping. First blood pressure. Then prostate. Now colon? I'm about sick of y'all.

The nurse scheduled the colonoscopy procedure. Listen, I'd never had one before and I didn't know what to expect. They gave me the prep. You know the prep; the one gallon of the nastiest liquid known to man and told me that I would need to fast from solid foods for a whole 24 hours. Just fluids.

I made jokes about this horrific lemon-flavored cocktail and the excessive trips to the bathroom. When I tell you, that fluid will shut any active lifestyle down.

The day of the procedure, I went on Facebook Live from the hospital bed, documenting much of the process.

But behind the humor was fear.

Fear of what they might find.

Fear of what might grow in silence.

And then comes the moment that no one wants to hear when you are waking up in the recovery room:

> *"Mr. Brown, we couldn't finish the procedure."*

What do you mean, you couldn't finish?

> *"There was too much stool in your system and if we had continued with the procedure, it could cause an infection or worse."*

The doctor went on to say,

> **"You're full of $#it and you'll have to come back."**

Well, that may not be exactly how he said it, but that is what I heard.

The Breakdown That Become a Breakthrough

Let me tell you something, when a doctor looks you in the eye and says anything related to,

> "You're too full of $#it for us to help you,"

that'll stop you cold.

I was literally blocked up. Backed up. And it was toxic.

And it hit me: this wasn't just physical.

It was spiritual. It was mental.

How many times do we walk around carrying what no longer serves us? Resentment. Regret. Old wounds. Dead-end jobs. Broken relationships. Childhood trauma. Bad habits. Institutional systems.

We say we're fine. We smile through it.
But the truth? We're full of it.

And it's not just old baggage. It's the emotional weeds that keep trying to root themselves. For me, it was self-doubt. That thing likes to pop up again and again, like a bad seed waiting for my attention. But I've learned that I cannot continue to water it. Instead, I had to switch my outlook and learn to pull and prune those weeds and put my energy into growing the things that bring me peace, purpose, and joy.

And just like that colon, our lives get so backed up that nothing can flow. The nutrients can't get through. The healing can't happen. And if we don't let it out, it poisons everything.

It made me think of a situation that I longed for. Even more, I had prayed for it. Yet I found out years later that the situation was not doing me any good. It was stressful. The people were spiteful. The atmosphere was tainted. The growth was stagnant. It took all I could to maintain. I had to make the decision that it wasn't worth it, and I had to let it go.

Oh, it was hard as I put everything into the project and organization. I had become sick to my stomach trying to keep it together and was willing to do so, but at what cost? It wasn't worth my health. My peace of mind. My name.

It appeared to me that I had to make the choice to let it go. I mean to truly walk away and release myself from that burden. I've heard people say that sometimes you will find yourself in thankless positions of power and influence, and this was one of those situations. Talk about a joy that came over me when I chose to walk away, it was unbelievable.

This letting go reminded me of something simple. Ever played with a water hose as a kid? Remember what happens when you clamp it shut with your thumb or bend the hose together. The pressure builds. The hose starts to bulge. Then when you let go, water sprays everywhere.

That's what it felt like. My body and my spirit were holding on to matters for much too long. Eventually, something's got to give.

A Community Reminder

After that first failed colonoscopy, I had to go back. This time I was better prepared, more cleansed, and emptier.

But something unexpected happened between appointments. A brother man reached out to me. He had seen my Facebook Live. He had been putting off his own screenings and medical advice. He had a tumor affecting his nose and vision. My public vulnerability pushed him to get checked out. And because of it, they caught something serious.

Hearing from him was a deeply rewarding moment. In some small way, I felt like I helped save a life. And that's when it really clicked: as men, we often get in our own way, thinking we can carry it all alone. But healing happens when we're open. When we share. When we learn from one another and walk each other toward the right path.

That's when I realized: This isn't just about me. This is about the **village**. This is about the **son that I have**. This was about my **transparency that might save somebody else's life.**

Release to Receive

The second time around, I prayed hard. My first prayer was that I never want to drink this disgusting fluid again. And did I mention that this time around, I had to enjoy **two gallons of the prescribed bowel prep polymer-based laxative known as polyethylene glycol** and become one with the toilet for two luxurious days on a liquid diet?

Oh, the joy! I am so glad I live by myself because it was not a pretty scene, nor a fragrant one. As for my second prayer, I was reminded of an old gospel song made popular by Rev. Ernest Davis, Jr. and the Wilmington/Chester Mass Choir that came to mind:

> *If You find anything that's not like You,*
> *I ask You Lord, You know what to do.*
> *Wash me Lord, cleanse me through and through…*
> *Take it away from me Lord, Take it away from me.*

As I was preparing to go LIVE for another Facebook Operating Room episode, I gave explicit instructions to the doctor:

> *"Do not wake me up under any circumstances unless you have finished the job. I don't care if you got to pump, prime, compress or even suction the stool out."*

At that point, I was ready to release it all. Ready or not, here it comes – and the medical team did what they were called to do. They cleaned me out, found the polyps, removed the dangerous ones, and gave me a fresh start.

I can't explain the relief I felt knowing I had passed through that moment; mentally, spiritually, and physically.

I know I'm not the only one who's ever felt stuck in "it," unsure of how to move forward. But that experience reminded me: *with the right kind of help, you can let it go.*

And letting it go can make room for something better.

When I first woke up, my only thought was, *"Where is the bathroom?"* Because I just knew another round was coming. But that feeling had soon passed away. Suddenly, I felt... light. The bloating was gone. My body felt unburdened, even though my rear end was a little sore. That moment reinforced it for me: **letting go always feels better than holding it in.**

What I have experienced wasn't just a physical reset, it was a **soul detox**. You can't just ask God to make room for blessings while you're still clinging to the blockages. You must let some things go. **Forgive. Surrender. Detox. Heal.**

The Deeper Lesson: Why We Hold On

So why do we stay full of it?

Because it's familiar.

Because it feels safer to carry what we know than to release what we can't control.

Because somewhere deep down, we're afraid of the emptiness. But listen to me: **Emptiness isn't the enemy. And neither is the beginning.** When I started losing weight, I didn't just shed pounds, I uncovered pain.

Guilt whispered that I had "cheated" by having surgery. I used to think that choosing a medical tool like weight loss surgery meant I hadn't earned the change. But healing taught me that a tool is still a tool whether it's surgery, therapy, or a treadmill. What matters most is that you choose yourself.

There was mental waste too. Worrying about being accepted by folks who didn't care about my health when I was struggling. I had to release that. The weight, the stress, the need for outside validation. I wasn't doing this for them. I was doing this for me. For the little boy in me who wanted to live.

Once I let go of the physical stuff, I cleansed my system. That was when I realized I had to do the same with my habits, my thinking, my fear, my shame. I had to deal with the stuff that clogged up my joy. The stuff that kept me from truly living. Letting go wasn't easy. But neither was holding on.

We're All Full of It

That's the real lesson.

We're all full of something.

Pain. Ego. Expectations. Guilt. Trauma.

Fear dressed up as ambition.

Shame disguised as pride.

But we don't have to stay that way.

We have the power to release it.

To surrender it.

To walk lighter.

To live freer.

More than once in my life I have had health scares that shook me. Just hearing the "C" word stirs up a storm inside of me. I've lost both my parents to some kind of cancer. When a doctor even begins to go there, my spirit tightens. My chest closes up. I begin to shut down. Though I know God has the final say, my trauma still speaks first.

That fear? It's real. And it became a wake-up call. I had to stop pretending I was invincible and a that I didn't have a cross to bear. I had to release unhealthy habits before they robbed me of breath, joy, or years I hadn't lived yet. Now, every day I do my work. You know a good gospel playlist can always get me moving. A quiet moment with God to center myself is a great time for me. And my therapist? What can I say about this man. He helps me unpack the thoughts that still hide in the corners. Every conversation with him feels like he is healing the younger me. You know, the one who was waiting to be heard, held, and healed.

So, I'll say it again:

We're all full of $#IT. And we gotta get it out.

Before it blocks our blessings.

Before it steals our breath.

Before it cost us our lives.

This journey is about more than health.

It's about **wholeness**.

It's not just about survival.

It's about **release**.

About **freedom**.

About choosing to live—**on purpose**.

Final Thought: The Courage to Release

Letting go is hard, but holding on can be heavier. Pain, pride, fear—if we don't release it, it builds up and blocks what we're meant to receive. Healing starts with honesty. You're not weak for needing help, you're wise to seek it.

What are you holding onto that's blocking your peace, your joy, or your health?

_____

_____

_____

Where in your life are you ignoring the warning signs spiritually, emotionally, or physically?

_____

_____

_____

What support systems (therapy, friendships, faith, wellness checks) can you lean into to begin your release?

_____

_____

_____

Your next chapter starts with what you're willing to let go of. Release the weight. Reclaim your breath. And walk forward lighter, freer, and finally ready.

Inspire Me Moment:
Secure Your Foundation

Every strong narrative begins with a solid foundation. The same is true in life and what you build with will determine the strength of what you create. Before stepping forward, take a moment to assess your foundation and ensure it is secure.

> *"Be careful who you build with because people will use you for the foundation and finish the structure with somebody else."*
> Gaus Ahamad

Reflection:
Not everyone you help build with will stay for the full construction. Some will take your strength, wisdom, and effort as their foundation—only to finish their masterpiece with someone else. And when that happens, it can feel like betrayal.

But here's the lesson: **You are not just a steppingstone.**

Be intentional about who you align yourself with. Build with those who not only recognize your contributions but value your presence in the process. The right partnerships don't just use your foundation, they grow with you, brick by brick.

Final Thought:
Your foundation is too valuable to be given away carelessly. **Protect it, strengthen it, and build with those who are worthy of the journey.**

Live Out Loud Challenge:
Secure Your Foundation

This challenge is about examining your boundaries, honoring your value, and protecting your peace.

Connect

Reach out to someone who has experienced burnout or betrayal because they gave too much without enough protection. Ask: **How did you rebuild your boundaries? What shifted about how you value your time, energy, and presence?**

Reflect

With a trusted peer, talk about where you've struggled to balance generosity and discernment. **Where have you poured out without protecting your own well-being?**

Support

Guide someone young or early in their journey to define their non-negotiables. Help them see that true generosity doesn't mean saying "yes" to everything. It means giving from a place of strength, not depletion.

Wellness Check-In
A Test of Faith & Healing

Purpose: When life shakes your foundation, this check-in helps you reconnect with your inner compass—aligning your mind, body, and soul to move through fear and uncertainty with faith.

Mind – The Compass: Where Am I Right Now?

Fear clouds the path. Take a moment to pause and ask yourself:

- What fear am I currently holding onto?
- What truth do I need to replace it with?

Direction Check:

"Faith is not the absence of fear—it's the decision to keep walking anyway."

Body – The Terrain: What Am I Feeling?

Fear often lives in the body—tight shoulders, shallow breath, racing heart. Take a deep breath. Place your hand on your chest. Inhale deeply, exhale slowly.

Try this:

- Slowly lift your arms as you inhale.
- Lower them as you exhale.
- Repeat with intention. Let tension go.

Grounding Reminder:

"This body has carried me through storms before. I am still standing."

Soul – The North Star: What Do I Believe?

Faith is the light that stays steady, even when the road is unclear. Repeat this affirmation aloud or in prayer:

"Even in my uncertainty, I trust that God is working on my behalf."

Reflection Prompt:

- What verse, quote, or mantra brings you peace when you can't see the outcome?

Spiritual Anchor:

"Healing is already happening—even when I can't feel it yet."

Final Word

You are walking through something difficult—but you're not walking alone. Let faith steady your steps, even if you're unsure where they're going. Keep moving. Healing is in motion.

The Inner Circle Club

**You've just stepped through something powerful.
Now it's time to speak on it and allow your "NET" Work!**

This is your space to connect, reflect, and build community with other readers.

CHAPTER 4: My Name Is Victory

- What fight are you in the middle of—and what's keeping you going?

- Have you ever confused being strong with being silent?

- What's your "third-day breakthrough" story?

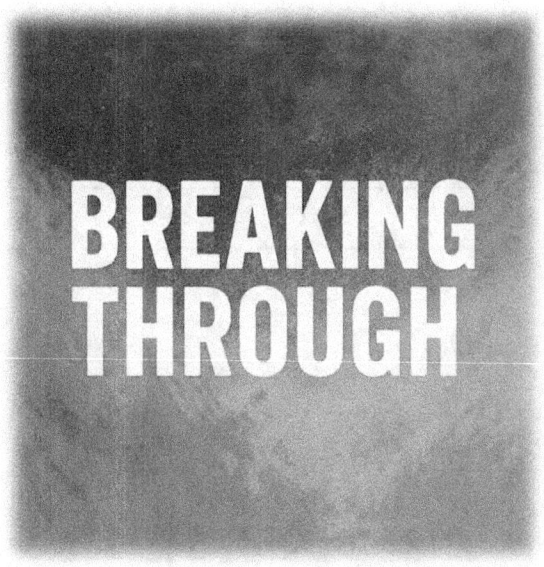

PART II:
BREAKING THROUGH

Theme: Healing, resilience, redefining masculinity, and spiritual growth

"You don't become strong because life was easy. You become strong because you decided not to give up."

Here, readers move from survival to transformation, confronting the hard truths and doing the deep inner work that leads to growth.

Take a deep breath. Release what no longer serves you. Center yourself in this moment. What are you sensing, thinking, or noticing? Let this page be your pause.

MINDFULNESS JOURNAL

DAY: MONTH: YEAR:

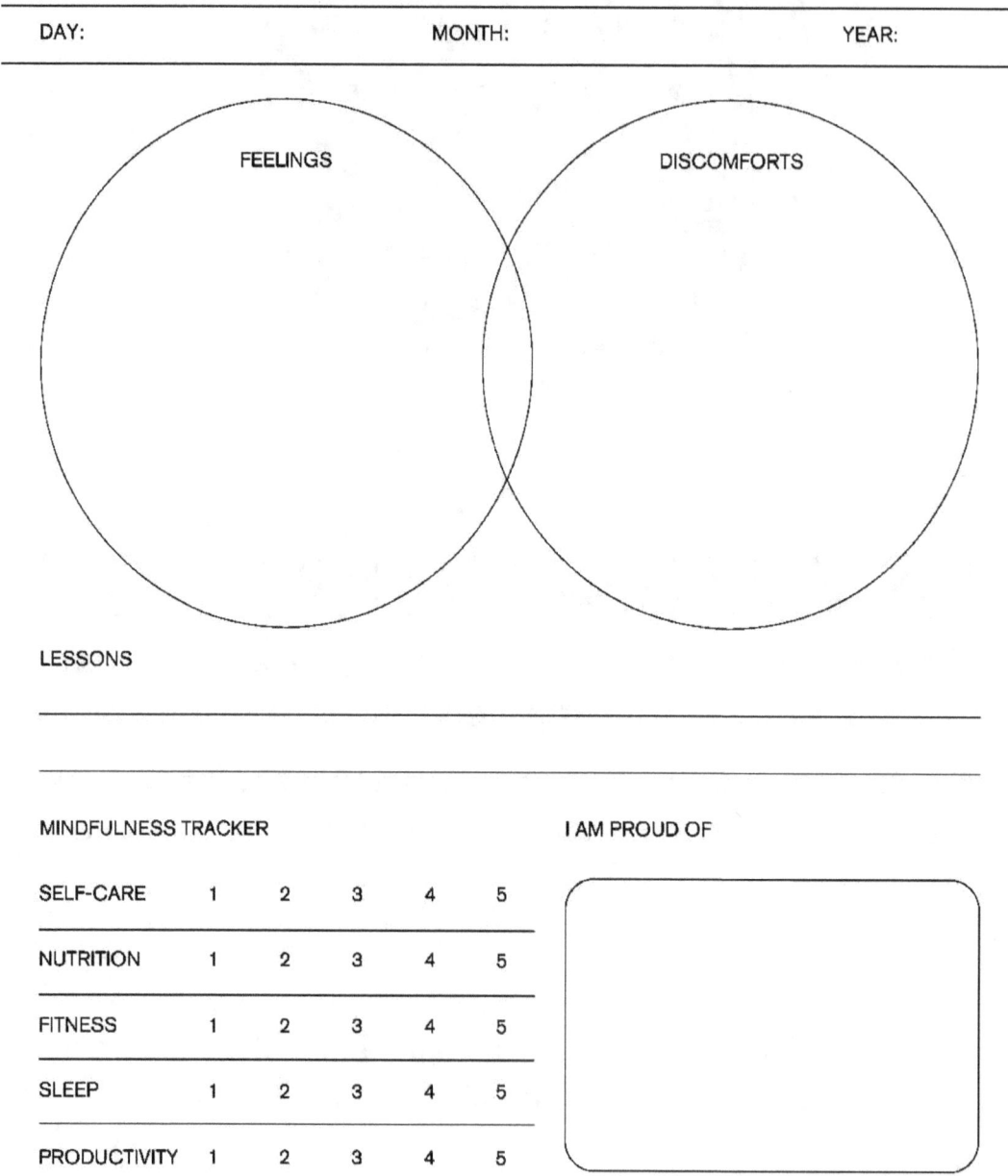

FEELINGS   DISCOMFORTS

LESSONS

MINDFULNESS TRACKER   I AM PROUD OF

SELF-CARE	1	2	3	4	5
NUTRITION	1	2	3	4	5
FITNESS	1	2	3	4	5
SLEEP	1	2	3	4	5
PRODUCTIVITY	1	2	3	4	5

CHAPTER 5:
REWRITING THE NARRATIVE

Opening Reflection

You think you know who you are—until someone you love tells you otherwise.

One moment, you're a child, heart wide open, believing love is unconditional, believing "family" means protection, acceptance, belonging. The next moment, a single sentence – sharp as glass – cuts you open.

Some wounds don't bleed on the outside. They bleed in the soul. Quiet. Invisible. Long after the words have faded.

This chapter isn't just about one denial. It's about the legacy of silence, the manipulation we inherit, and the exhausting search for a seat at the table. It's about the parts of ourselves we bury to be accepted—and what it takes to reclaim them.

It's also about unexpected grace. The brother I never knew. The love I kept showing, even when it wasn't returned. The forgiveness I gave, even when it wasn't asked for. This isn't a clean story tied up with a bow. It's messy. It's complicated. It's real.

But if you're willing to walk into the wreckage with me, you'll see: Somewhere in the broken pieces, we don't just find our story, we rewrite it.

Welcome to the place where survival turns into strength.
Where being denied doesn't destroy you.
It defines the champion you're becoming.

The Times My Father Changed My Life

The Father I Knew vs. The Father I Wanted

Let me tell you about a time when my world was turned upside down. I had to be about 8 years old, visiting my father's house. You must understand that I didn't grow up living with him. I knew who he was, but I didn't live with him. I knew he had another family, and I came in between that dynamic. There was always this unspoken tension—like I was welcome, but only up to a point. Like love had limits I didn't understand yet.

And yet, there were moments that felt so normal they almost made me forget the gaps. Like waking up on a Saturday morning and finding him at the kitchen table in a bathrobe, eating a bowl of Frosted Flakes and watching cartoons like nothing was broken. Or knowing that if I ever needed a pair of black church socks, I could sneak into my mom's room and open a particular dresser drawer. Inside, there would be a few pairs of socks, t-shirts, underwear— and that familiar scent of Aramis cologne. That smell always stopped me. For a brief second, it was like he was still there. Maybe he hadn't left after all.

It was confusing—how someone could be so close and still feel so far away. That was the father I knew. But the father I longed for? He wasn't just the man passing through moments. He was something more solid, more steady. I didn't have the words for it back then, but I knew enough to feel the contradiction—how he could be with us on any random morning yet belong to a life that didn't include me every day.

As a child, I couldn't make sense of how he could sit in our house, eat our food, watch TV, send me off to bed, when I knew he had another home. Another life. It left me wondering where I really fit. If I was part of the picture—or just penciled in around the edges.

That kind of emotional limbo—being close, but not fully claimed— did something to me. It planted questions I didn't know how to ask and feelings I didn't know how to name. I carried that uncertainty into every part of my young life, trying to make sense of where I belonged and who I was supposed to be. And sometimes, that confusion showed up in the smallest, most ordinary moments.

The Maury Povich Show

One day, I was playing at the playground with my sister, she's about a year and a half younger than me. We were having a good time. Like many siblings, as it often goes, we got into a tit-for-tat situation. She was on the swings, and I wanted to swing. Of course, it was my turn, and when she wouldn't budge, I pushed her off.

She was upset and, as siblings often do, ran inside to tell our dad. But I wasn't worried. I figured, "Tell him, he's my dad too." I didn't think much of it at the time, but the tension between us was building, as we grew up not really acknowledging each other as siblings, though we were, by blood.

We both ran to the house to find my father sitting with some of his friends in the basement, chatting and laughing. My sister burst into her complaint, and I tried to tell my side of the story. But then, my father looked at both of us and said,

"Alright, I need you both to stop all this arguing."

And then, in a moment, this single act would damage me forever.

My sister looked up and said,

> *"Daddy, tell him he's not your father."*

I'll never forget the coldness in his eyes as he said, like an episode from an afternoon reality TV talk show,

> **"I am not his father."**

My world shattered in that instant. It was as if the ground underneath me disappeared. I was devastated. To hear him deny me like that— someone I had been looking up to all my life—was something I wasn't prepared for. I remember wanting to pack my bags and go home. I wanted to leave, but somehow, I stayed.

From that moment on, I had to learn how to adjust. I had to learn how to adapt to a world where my identity was now in question. In one moment, my world was forever changed.

Years went by, and though I would often visit, the emotional scars of those words stayed with me. The man I idolized – who is my father – had denied me in front of the one person I wanted to prove myself to. But even in the wake of that painful moment, life kept moving. So did we. And somehow, so did our bond, however fragile it may have felt.

Sibling Tensions, Sibling Love

After that day in the basement, after those five words cracked something open in me – my relationship with Ericka changed. Not in an explosive way, but in a subtle, quiet way. There was a tension that wasn't there before, an invisible thread pulling at our bond. Still, despite everything, I was determined not to give up on her. I held onto the hope that we could still be the kind of siblings who showed up for each other.

And truthfully, we had our moments. The kind of moments that only siblings understand—where chaos and laughter live side by side. I remember one summer road trip with our dad and all the kids. We had checked into a Howard Johnson's somewhere down South. Swimming was on the agenda for the day and trust me, Ericka and I loved to swim. Our dad had made sure we learned how from a young age. But right before we were about to head to the pool, a monster-sized horsefly found its way into our hotel room. It buzzed through the air like it had something to prove, and then – just my luck – it landed right on Ericka.

Naturally, I jumped into hero mode to save her.

I grabbed the flyswatter with the bold confidence of a big brother and swung to save the day. I missed the fly—but managed to tag her *real* good. All I remember after that is yelling, crying, and a whole lot of drama. The result? We were both punished and banned from the pool while our brothers splashed around having the time of their lives. Typical us.

That was our rhythm. Fighting one moment, cracking jokes the next. Even after that moment in the basement, we still found ways to stay connected, whether it was high school hangouts, going to parties, or just clowning with our mixed group of friends. We never talked about the day I got denied. Not directly. But I always hoped she knew how badly I wanted to just be her brother. Fully. Out loud. No qualifiers.

I never forgot the words she said that day. And I'll be honest, sometimes I still wonder if she ever thought about what they did to me. But I also remember the times she *did* show up for me. Like at our brother Sumlor Jr.'s funeral, when someone asked if I was her husband, and she replied,

> *"This is my father's other son."*

That might not sound like much, but in that moment, I felt seen. Acknowledged.

There were layers to our relationship—complicated, messy, and mostly unspoken. But there was love, even if it came wrapped in sarcasm and side-eyes. In my family, love didn't always sound like "I love you." Sometimes it showed up in silence, or in the moments you least expected. That pattern didn't stop with my sister; it stayed in my relationship with my father. The same man who once denied me now asked me to ride beside him. So, when Clifford died, and someone needed to identify the body, he called me.

The Road to Arkansas

We drove in silence. Me, my father, and a farting dog. From Ohio to Arkansas to Texas, retracing the final steps of the son he claimed in public... and the one he hid in the back.

Clifford was gone. Found alone from an asthma attack in Little Rock. And someone had to go identify the body. My father chose me to ride with him, and maybe that should have meant something. Maybe it did. But the silence between us was louder than the grief.

It was a strange, uncomfortable road trip; physically, emotionally, spiritually. The car reeked of regret and unspoken words. The dog, bless her little soul, passed gas the entire time like some awkward punctuation to the spaces we didn't know how to fill. My father barely spoke, and when he did, it was about logistics, not loss. There was no, "How are you holding up, son?" Just a quiet mission to collect a body and follow Clifford's journal like a breadcrumb trail through his final days.

I remember somewhere outside of Dallas, I'd had enough. By this point, we had named the body, retrieved his personal effects, and even found the U-Store-It facility and shipped all of his other belongings home. I turned to my father and said, "Just take me to the airport. I'll fly home." He didn't respond, he just kept driving. It was as if grief had frozen something in him—and maybe it had. He didn't know how to process losing Clifford. Truth is, none of us did.

But what made it worse was what came after. When we finally got home, the family gathered for the funeral. Except I wasn't really part of the family, not in the way that counted. I wasn't allowed to sit with them. I wasn't asked to help with the arrangements. Yet, I was expected to show up, stay quiet, and grieve from the sidelines.

Clifford was the only one who had ever publicly embraced me. And even in death, I couldn't stand beside him as a brother. That pain… that exile… it cut deep.

It wasn't the first time I'd been excluded. It wouldn't be the last. But that trip, those quiet highways, the stale pit stop diners, the heavy grief, the dog that wouldn't stop passing gas, it etched itself into me. Not because of the absurdity, but because of the clarity: I was both needed and denied in the same breath. Chosen for the journey, but not for the seat at the table. Still, even in that space of emotional exile, time had a way of shifting things. What I didn't expect was how life would eventually draw us closer again.

That trip wasn't just about grief, it was a journey through silence, exile, and the kind of clarity that only loss can bring. One of the clearest examples of that came years later – on a long, quiet road trip I'll never forget. It was on that trip that some of the deepest unspoken truths surfaced not through conversation, but through silence.

Shifting Perceptions and Surprising Revelations

Fast forward to adulthood. My father's health began to decline. He was diagnosed with prostate cancer, unbeknownst to anyone in the family. I was already an adult at this point, but it wasn't until I was away at a Bethune-Cookman homecoming event that I found out how serious things had gotten. My sister had come to the city while I was out of town, and found him at home unresponsive, so she took him to the hospital.

After a series of tests and examinations, we found out—my father had stage 4 cancer. The news hit me hard. I didn't understand how it had gotten so bad so quickly. My question to the medical team, "What happened to stages 1, 2, and 3?" My father had been silent about it, not wanting to burden anyone. But here I was, at this point in my life, with the same man who had once denied me, now in the fight of his life.

His decline was rapid. From the time my sister had him admitted to the hospital, he stayed until he transitioned. At this point, I was there with him as much as I could be. One day, we were watching a

Cleveland Browns game in the hospital dining room, just after Thanksgiving. The Browns were not doing so well that season when he said to me, "I'm ready to go." I took him back to his room and he said it again, "I'm ready to go." Those words stuck with me, and less than a day later, he passed away.

I thought the hardest part of this journey was over. But the funeral would hold one final surprise that would rewrite the story I thought I knew.

A Funeral Revelation: The Unexpected Discovery

But life had one more surprise for me. At the funeral home, while I was dealing with the emotional toll of my father's passing, something completely unexpected happened. Two men walked up to me – one I recognized, the other I didn't. I asked how he knew my dad. The stranger introduced himself and said,

"He's my father too."

I stood there in shock, staring at this man who looked like he could be a long-lost relative. He bore a striking resemblance to Sumlor Jr. My first reaction was disbelief. Was this a joke? Am I being pranked? But then he shared details that I couldn't confirm or deny yet sounded entirely plausible. And just like that, I found out I had a brother.

Until that moment, I thought I knew the full lineup of my father's children. Gregory Peek was the oldest, born to a different mother, and had passed away years ago. Then came Sumlor Harris, Jr. and Clifford Harris – both sons of Jean – who also preceded our father in death. I came next, followed by our sister Ericka, also Jean's daughter. But meeting Tim Bishop that day shifted everything. From what I could gather, he was older than me, possibly right after Clifford, making him the fourth of six. His mother wasn't Jean or mine, adding another twist to our already tangled family story.

Just then, my son's mother walked in. She had been with me throughout the process. I turned to her and said, "You're not going to believe this." I pointed to the man and asked, "Who does he look like?" She smiled and said, "He looks just like Sumlor Jr." In that moment, I realized, I wasn't just losing a father, I was gaining a brother.

It was surreal. I didn't know how to process the revelation, but one thing was clear: family is more than just blood. Sometimes, we discover bonds in the most unexpected ways.

In the end, I went from the boy denied by his father to the man who gained a brother at his father's funeral. Life is full of surprises sometimes the kind that help us heal and move forward.

Final Thought: The Journey of Family & Identity

Sometimes, the family you think you know can surprise you in ways you never expected.

The relationships that shape you aren't always the ones you've grown up with, they can come at unexpected times and in unexpected forms.

What part of your family dynamic is due for a fresh perspective?

_____

_____

_____

What bonds have you yet to explore that could bring unexpected healing into your life?

_____

_____

_____

How can you be open to the idea that family is not only about blood, but about connection, support, and understanding?

_____

_____

Embrace the surprising connections that life offers. Your journey is about what's still ahead. Let's walk through it together.

Identity and Family Dynamics

Who Am I?

Growing up, love wasn't just a feeling – it was survival. My family ran a minority enterprise; AAA Check Checking of Ohio, Something Fishy To Go, Boss's Beverage, Club 66, The Sir-RAH House (to name a few) in Cleveland with multiple locations, so crossing paths was inevitable. My father, my brothers, my mother, their mother, and my sister all worked together. During that, I often found myself asking, *"Where do I fit?"* Torn between being a son, a worker, and a brother, I struggled to find a place that felt truly mine.

The business wasn't just about work; it was a constant test of identity and relationship. Imagine being a young boy, surrounded by family but still feeling like an outsider. While we all worked side by side, we didn't always see each other clearly. That disconnect wasn't new, it was inherited. Passed down through choices and circumstances set in motion long before I arrived.

As I got older, that sense of displacement only deepened. I tried to live up to the role's others had written for me, but my identity was constantly shifting. It wasn't until adulthood that I began to understand how deeply that confusion had shaped me.

Still, I loved my "other" family fiercely. I found joy in the work we did together, even when it cost me peace. I embraced the purpose, even when the dynamics were complicated. But the hardest part? Not knowing who I was beneath all the roles. Was I just the son of the owner? Was I a brother? Or was I simply the boy they made space for—but never fully claimed?

Those questions stayed with me. Especially in the business, where job titles didn't always come with trust – or truth.

Identity Dynamics: The Struggle to Understand Who I Am

The family business mirrored the emotional tension I lived with daily. We didn't share a home, but we shared a workload. And in that space, the lines between family and function blurred. Everyone else seemed to have a clear role. I was still searching.

Working beside my father and siblings wasn't just a task, it was an identity trial. I didn't belong to one household. I wasn't fully "his." In his home, I often felt like the guest. The "charity case." Not the son.

So, in the business, I wore every hat – worker, son, helper – but none of them felt like they fit. The expectations were heavy, but the silence was heavier. Especially when it came to the one word I longed to say – and wasn't allowed to: *Dad.*

The Hidden Pain: Identity Struggling in Silence

One of the most painful aspects of this dynamic was the simple act of being told, at the age of four, I couldn't call my father "Dad." I had to refer to him by his first name "Sumlor" or "Mr. Harris." As a child, I couldn't understand why something so simple, so fundamental to a father-son relationship, was kept from me. Every time I said "Dad," I was punished or scolded. This single act fractured my sense of identity in ways I couldn't fully grasp at the time.

I couldn't express the hurt I felt, but it became something I carried with me every single day. Watching other children call their fathers "Dad" with warmth and affection only deepened my sense of loss. My father distanced himself from the father-son relationship I so desperately longed for, and that pain followed me into adulthood.

As I grew older, I began to understand that my father's actions were his way of setting boundaries—whether they were right or wrong. What I didn't realize was that I had inherited much more from him than I knew. My mannerisms, my style, even the way I spoke—I looked more like him than anyone else in the family. My mom even wanted to give me his last name, but at the time, the hospital wouldn't allow it, so my middle name is how I carry his name.

Even with this physical resemblance, I still struggled with feelings of displacement. But eventually, as I began to grow and gain confidence, I realized that I had been suppressing my identity for years, trying to meet everyone else's expectations while not fully understanding who I was.

Inherited Patterns

The deeper I looked into my identity, the more I realized how much of it was shaped not just by who my father was—but by the patterns he passed down. Some of those patterns were quiet, embedded in how decisions were made, how affection was withheld, and how power showed up in relationships. Others were bold and manipulative, shaping the paths of everyone around him—including my mother.

Before I was born, my mom was on her own path. A proud student at John Hay High School in Cleveland, she had dreams, goals, and direction. But from what I understand, my father began courting her before she even finished high school. My grandmother knew about it, saw it unfolding and said nothing. But from what I've been told, she may have gotten caught up in the sweet talk and financial flash that surrounded him. And so, she allowed it to happen.

After high school, my mother began building her future. She secured a job as a bookkeeper at NASA Glenn Research Center. Later, during the early years when the Ohio Lottery was first established, she earned a position there as well. She was working, taking classes at Cuyahoga Community College, and laying the foundation for something big.

He convinced her to walk away from it all. To leave behind the steady job, school, and personal growth for a different kind of life. The life that revolved around him. She became his partner in business, in family, and in all the complicated, blurry spaces in between. Some might call it a work-wife situation. Others might call it survival. But from what I can gather, she was a woman whose light was dimmed in service of someone else's hustle. Then on May 2, 1970, I arrived. The living proof of a love story that was never quite whole. A child born from passion, persuasion, and a promise that never fully came to pass.

What I've come to realize is that his manipulation didn't start with me. It was generational. It was strategic. It was wrapped in charm, control, and conditional love. The same kind of persuasive pull my mother experienced, abandoning her dreams in service to someone else's vision would show up in my life too, just in different packaging.

I saw it again when Clifford's daughter, Cierra, was told by what seemed to be both my dad and Jean that she couldn't call me "Uncle Anthony" or my wife at the time "Aunt Tasha." Just like I wasn't allowed to call him "Dad," she wasn't allowed to call me "family." Same script. Different cast. Another attempt to draw lines that kept people separated instead of connected.

That's the thing about inherited patterns; they don't just live in the past. They show up in how we speak, how we love, how we choose or refuse to claim one another. And if we're not intentional, we end up living out the very stories we swore we'd never repeat.

These patterns of distancing, of redefining love through control had shaped so much of my childhood. But adulthood finally gave me a chance to break the cycle.

Shifting Identity and Learning to Adjust

As I entered adulthood, the need to constantly adjust and fit in began to fade. But that process wasn't without its challenges. The key to growth was learning to adjust in ways that didn't compromise who I was. I couldn't keep hiding from myself, the hurts, and the struggles. My father had emotionally distanced himself from me, and now I had to learn how to navigate life without allowing that distance to define me.

I knew my father loved me, but his way of showing love wasn't always clear to me. While other kids got to experience their fathers at sporting events or school functions, I often received material things as signs of affection. When my brothers got a new bike, I got one too. When they got new clothes, I got a credit card. It was his way, but I longed for something deeper.

As "bell hooks" (2000) so powerfully writes in All About Love,

"To know love we have to invest time and commitment."

Growing up, I mistook silence for strength and gifts for affection. I needed more than provision—I needed presence. It took years to understand that real love is not about what's given but how it's shared.

Eventually, I realized that all the struggles, the confusion, and the uncertainty about my identity were part of the journey. Life didn't give me a clear path, but what it gave me was the ability to adjust. I had to find my place, not just in the family business, but in the world, as a man and as an individual.

Honor in the Face of Denial

People often ask me why I stayed. Why did I keep coming around after that moment in the basement? Why I cared for a man who once looked me in the eye and denied being my father. The answer isn't simple, but it's real: I didn't want to lose what little I did have.

See, I was raised to stay in a child's place. To hold my tongue. To respect authority. And in our world, his word was law. Questioning it wasn't just discouraged, it was dangerous. But deeper than that, I craved his acceptance. I didn't want to push him so far that I lost even the scraps of relationship I was clinging to. So, I adjusted. I stayed quiet. I played the role.

There was also something spiritual that kept me tethered. My grandmother made sure I was grounded in the Word, and when the

Bible says, "Honor thy father and thy mother," I took that to heart. I didn't always understand what that looked like, especially when the person you're trying to honor doesn't always honor you in return. But I did it. I stayed. I served. I showed up. Even when it hurts.

But let's be honest, the hurt ran deep. It didn't stop at the basement. It showed up later in ways I didn't expect. After college, while working for the family, I landed a part-time gig at a radio station. It was small, but full of promise. It was a foot in the door towards a promising career in the media field, something I was enthusiastic about. I could see a path forward. I could feel the momentum.

But my father, ever the persuader, convinced me to stay in the family business. He dangled the idea that one day I would take over. If I stayed loyal, if I stayed committed, the legacy would be mine. I chose loyalty over ambition. I let go of my dream of pursuing a radio or television career, thinking I was investing in something greater. That someday, I would be seen as more than just "the other son." That I would finally be confirmed.

That day never came.

I never took over the business. What I did take on, though, was a front-row seat to the emotional toll of trying to belong in a space that never fully made room for me. And still, I stayed.

Because honoring him didn't mean erasing the past, it meant refusing to let the past make me bitter. I chose to walk in forgiveness, even when it felt undeserved. I chose to keep showing up, not for approval, but for peace. For me.

> *"Get rid of all bitterness... forgiving each other, just as in Christ God forgave you."* — **Ephesians 4:31–32**

It didn't mean forgetting. It meant releasing what no longer served me. That scripture became more than a verse—it became my vow.

Forgiveness wasn't approval—it's survival.

Forgiveness wasn't optional—it was oxygen.

Holding bitterness had suffocated my joy long enough.

Shifting Perceptions: Growing Into My True Self

As I grew older, I finally realized that I didn't need to suppress myself anymore. I didn't need to wear the mask of "not being good enough" just to fit into a world that wasn't ready for me to be fully seen. I began to understand that my identity wasn't defined by anyone else. It was shaped by the decisions I made, the courage to step into my own life, and the acknowledgment that I had the right to define myself.

The journey to becoming my true self wasn't easy or immediate. It took a shift in mindset, a realization that I had been playing a role I didn't need to play anymore. My place in the family business didn't define me, nor did my father's rejection of me as his "son." I was more than what had been imposed on me.

Breaking Free: Embracing the Journey of Self-Discovery

One of the most powerful steps I took was allowing myself to be vulnerable. Confronting the complicated relationship, I had with my father was painful, but it was necessary. There came a point when I reached my boiling point. At work, I lost it. I couldn't keep being told to stay in my place or be quiet. I needed everyone to understand that I just wanted to be accepted for who I was. The man who had always tried to keep me quiet through material gifts and avoidance had to know that I wasn't going to be silenced anymore.

That moment of vulnerability was the beginning of my healing. I made peace with my identity and embraced the journey that had led me to this point. It wasn't just the family business or the strained relationship with my father, it was all part of my story. But moving forward didn't mean forgetting. It meant choosing forgiveness, even when the pain had every right to stay.

And that choice, one my mother never stopped believing I could make, opened the door to something I never expected: reconciliation.

Forgiveness: The Final Gift

My mother always hoped we would find our way back to each other. Despite all the tension, the denial, the silence, and the scars, she believed in redemption. She believed there could still be love where there had once been pain. And in the end, she was right.

We didn't get there through some picture-perfect breakthrough moment. We didn't hug it out and suddenly become the father and son I had once imagined we could be. But we found peace in our own way. Through the blowups, the misunderstandings, the long silences, and even the small, quiet gestures, something in our relationship began to shift. We were no longer pretending. We were just... real.

There was something humbling about seeing him in his most vulnerable state. He was no longer the towering man who could silence a room with a look, but a man facing his own mortality. The father who once denied me was now being cared for by the very son he once refused to claim. And yet, I didn't withhold my love. I honored him until his last breath. Not just because he earned it. But because I chose it.

He did the best he could. That's what I tell myself now. He made choices that hurt me, yes. But he also showed up in his own way. He taught me things. Sometimes through his presence, and sometimes through his absence. And in the end, I got to know the man who gave me life. Not the myth. Not the legend. Not the image. Just the man.

We didn't fix everything, but we did enough. Enough to close the chapter. Enough to lay down the pain.

I don't carry the pain anymore. I carry the lessons.
And that—for me—is the final gift.

Final Thought: Embracing Your Identity

Sometimes, we are forced to navigate through life without a clear sense of direction. It's easy to get caught up in the expectations placed upon us, the labels others try to give us, and the struggles that seem to define us. But in the end, the journey of self-discovery is about letting go of all those external influences and truly understanding who we are.

What parts of your identity are you holding onto because of others' expectations?

_____

_____

_____

How can you redefine your sense of self-independence in the roles that were given to you?

_____

_____

_____

What does it look like for you to fully embrace who you are, without apology?

_____

_____

_____

The journey of family and identity is never easy, but it is yours to take.

Inspire Me Moment:
Good Over Nice

Rewriting your story requires discernment—understanding what aligns with your values and what merely looks appealing. The world will present many 'nice' options, but only a few will truly be good for you. As you turn the page, commit to choosing what serves your highest purpose.

"Nice is different than good."
Stephen Sondheim

Reflection:
Don't be fooled into thinking that everything "nice" is meant for you. Sometimes, what's truly good for you won't always look flashy or make sense to everyone else.

Think about shopping for clothes. You might see something that looks great on the hanger, but once you try it on, it doesn't fit right. Life works the same way. Just because something seems appealing doesn't mean it's right for you.

The world often values appearance over substance. But what's truly good for you will stand the test of time. It takes self-awareness to know what aligns with your values and purpose.

Final Thought:
Not everything that shines belong in your life. Trust yourself to choose what's good over what's just nice—because the right fit will always feel like home.

Live Out Loud Challenge:
Good Over Nice

True growth isn't about seeking approval. It's about standing firmly in what's right. This challenge calls you to prioritize goodness over surface-level niceness, choosing authenticity, courage, and alignment every time.

Connect

Talk with a mentor, elder, or role model about a time they had to make a hard but right decision. Ask: **"How did you know it was time to stop pleasing and start protecting your purpose?"**

Reflect

With a trusted friend or peer, discuss a moment when saying "yes" to yourself meant saying "no" to others. What inner compass guided you? How did it feel to stand in your truth, even if it wasn't popular?

Support

Help someone younger or newer on the journey explore what values matter most to them. Show them how to use those values as a compass. Be the one that helps them walk boldly, choose wisely, and live authentically, no matter who's watching.

Wellness Check-In
Rewriting the Narrative

Purpose: This check-in is your reminder: the pen is in your hands. Honor where you've been. Let go of what no longer serves you. Write the truth of who you're becoming.

Dear Me,

You've been holding onto stories shaped by fear, pain, and people who couldn't see your worth. But today, you will take the pen back.

You are not your mistakes.
You are not the lie that says you're not enough.
You are not stuck—you're still becoming.

Take a breath.
Look yourself in the mirror and say it:
"I am not my past. I'm writing a new story—on my own terms."

Now tear up the old page.
Release it.
And begin again—with love, with truth, with strength.

Journal Prompts

- What's one limiting belief you're ready to rewrite?
- What truth will guide your next chapter?
- If your life were a book, what's the title of your next chapter?

Final Word

You are the author and the main character. Write boldly. Write honestly. And let it be a story that reflects who you truly are.

The Inner Circle Club

**You've just stepped through something powerful.
Now it's time to speak on it and allow your "NET" Work!**

This is your space to connect, reflect, and build community with other readers.

CHAPTER 5: Rewriting the Narrative

- What parts of your story have you had to rewrite for yourself?

- Who told you who you were—and how did you unlearn it?

- How do you hold space for complicated family truths?

CHAPTER 6:
WHAT FORGIVENESS FREES

Opening Reflection

Some wounds aren't visible. They don't bleed. They don't scar the skin. But they are heavy enough to break a man from the inside out.

The day after my mother passed, the world kept spinning—but mine stood still. The grief was suffocating. The loneliness was deafening. And the silence inside my mind was louder than any storm outside.

That wasn't the first time I carried invisible weight. It started years ago before the hospital visits, before the funeral arrangements, before the final goodbyes. It started with the quiet battles no one sees: the slow erosion of joy, the sleepless nights, the fake smiles, the whispered prayers. I had spent a lifetime learning how to "push through"—how to hide pain behind achievement, how to wear strength like a mask.

But mental health doesn't negotiate with pride.

It doesn't care how strong you pretend to be.

It will find you.

It will sit with you.

And if you don't face it, it will eventually consume you.

This chapter is not about pretending.

It's about confronting what we've been taught to avoid.

It's about admitting that sometimes faith and therapy go hand-in-hand.

It's about shattering the stigma that says seeking help is weakness.

It's about realizing that healing doesn't happen in hiding—it happens in honesty.

We don't just carry the weight for ourselves.

We carry it for the generations who were told to suffer in silence.

We carry it for the young people who think they have to face life alone.

We carry it for the family members we lost because they couldn't find the words or the help in time.

This is the chapter where we break the silence. Where we lay the burdens down.

Where we stop pretending, we're fine and start building the strength that only truth can offer.

Not every superhero wears a cape.

Sometimes, the bravest thing you can do is whisper:

"I need help."

The Day After September 20, 2020

Losing My First Girlfriend

Yesterday was heavy. And by yesterday, I mean the day I lost my mom. I remember the phone call, the words that broke me into pieces. But that wasn't the first time I had faced loss. I had already buried a part of me when my father passed, and yet, nothing could prepare me for the heaviness of this moment.

I had just come to terms with the fact that I would soon have to let go. My mom had been in the hospital for some time, and on that Friday before, she said to me, "I'm tired." Those two words hit me like a freight train. They weren't just a statement; they were a surrender. She knew. I knew. It was time.

She had prepared everything—her obituary, her arrangements—years ahead. She even wanted me to make sure her sister could be there for the funeral. She was ready.

But even though I knew she was ready, the pain hit differently. She had been my constant, my rock, the one who always had my back, even when I didn't deserve it. And now, I had to face a world without her physical presence. But in the stillness of that loss, something else began to rise—memories, teachings, and the quiet realization that her legacy was already woven into me.

The Moment of Realization: Legacy and Life Lessons

What struck me the hardest was how she had lived her life and how much of her strength she had passed down to me. I wasn't just mourning the loss of a mother; I was mourning the loss of a legacy.

Her sense of style was unmatched. She coordinated everything—whether it was the way she set the dinner table or how she would serve in the ministry. There was always purpose in her actions, and she did everything with intention. That flair for life, the ability to bring people together, and the belief in delivering your best every single time—those were the lessons I carried with me.

I wasn't just losing my mom. I was losing the guiding force that had shaped me into who I was becoming. The woman who taught me how to carry myself with grace, strength, and determination was gone, and I was left to carry that legacy forward.

The day she passed, I had no words. I wanted to scream at the sky, but all I could do was sit there in the hospital, broken, wondering how I could continue without her guidance. But the truth is, I had been prepared to live without her—whether I knew it or not. She had been preparing me all along.

I think about the times when she would fuss at me, then telling me how proud she was of my accomplishments, even when I didn't think they were worth celebrating. I think about the times she told me how she believed in me, even when I couldn't see it for myself. And now, I had to carry that legacy. Still, preparation doesn't soften the blow. Grief came in like a storm I wasn't ready for, carrying guilt, confusion, and an ache I couldn't name.

The Hidden Weight of Grief

After her passing, I was in a state of emotional overload. I felt a deep sense of loss, confusion, and guilt. I remember feeling like I had failed her in some way. I wondered if there was more, I could have done, if I could have been there more for her. I carried that guilt for a while, feeling unworthy of her love and care. This loss hit me in ways I didn't expect. It was so much worse than the divorce or the loss of my father. I literally lost my mind.

The thing with grief is, you don't just lose a person, you lose parts of yourself. You realize how intertwined you were with that person. Their presence had shaped you, molded you, and without them, you feel a part of you is missing too. My personal identity had been so tied to my mother's influence that I wasn't sure who I was without her.

That kind of loss doesn't disappear. It lingers. But over time, I began to learn that healing is possible even if it's slow, uneven, and full of setbacks.

Grief and Healing: A Gradual Process

Over the months that followed, I began to realize that the person I was becoming was also shaped by what she had instilled in me. I couldn't keep hiding from myself or grief. Slowly, I started to accept it. Therapy helped. But there were still dark days. Days when I couldn't pull myself out of bed, or I struggled to see a way forward. The first few holidays were especially hard. Christmas was not just about the family; it was about the void she left.

In 2024, I made the decision to join my family for Thanksgiving in Atlanta, something I hadn't done in years. My son, who lives in New York, came too. It was the first time in years that I felt her presence of love and connection during the holidays. That moment marked a significant continuation of my healing journey, even though I didn't realize it at the time. The support of family during this difficult period was invaluable. They refused to let me suffer alone, forcing me out of my isolation. It was through their persistence that I began to heal.

And in that healing, I started to rediscover her—not just in memories, but in my actions, my purpose, and the way I choose to show up in the world.

Legacy: How I Carry Her with Me

My mother's legacy lives on in me. She always wanted to see people celebrate life, to appreciate those around them while they still could. And that's what I strive to do—show love, give encouragement, and appreciate the people in my life. I even carry her song, *Give Me My Flowers* by James Cleveland, as a reminder to celebrate others while they are still here. My mission now is to honor her by doing the things she taught me: embracing the present, showing love, and lifting others up.

But as I think about the future, I realize that the struggles, the loss, and the uncertainty of who I was are all part of the process. Life is messy, and we don't always have control over our path. But I do have control over how I choose to walk it—how I honor the legacy that's been passed to me, and how I choose to carry that forward.

Final Thought: The Power of Legacy and Healing

Loss is an inevitable part of life, but it doesn't have to define us. We don't have to carry the weight of grief forever.
In fact, we can use the lessons from those we've lost to propel us forward.

What legacy has been passed down to you that continues to shape your life?

_____

_____

_____

How can you embrace the parts of you that are rooted in love, even after loss?

_____

_____

_____

What steps can you take today to begin your journey toward healing and embracing your full identity?

_____

_____

_____

Grief may take its toll, but we can choose to honor those who came before us by carrying their legacy and walking through the pain to find peace.

Breaking the Stigma

Navigating the Invisible Struggle

Mental health isn't just a trending topic. It's real. It's personal. And for too long, we didn't talk about it. On a particular morning, I found myself walking around the campus of Johnson C. Smith University in Charlotte, NC. The warm, humid air wrapped around me as the sounds of the marching band practicing in the distance brought me back to familiar memories of college life. There's something about being on an HBCU campus that feels like a sacred, grounding experience—one that reminds me of where I come from and why I do what I do.

But this walk wasn't just about nostalgia. It was about mental health. It was about depression, anxiety, and the toll it takes on young people today. As I walked across campus, I saw students hurrying to class, some laughing, others buried in their phones. I couldn't help but wonder: How many of them are silently struggling? How many of them are walking through their day without anyone knowing what they're truly going through?

That's when I ran into Charmaine, a student from Cleveland, OH at Johnson C. Smith. I had taught her in high school, and now here she was— a college senior, a new member of Sigma Gamma Rho, and seemingly thriving.

But when we started talking, she admitted something that took me by surprise.

"It's been rough," she said, looking down before meeting my gaze. *"Being so far from home… I don't have family here. It gets lonely. The stress, the anxiety hits harder when you don't have a strong support system close by."*

Her words hit me deep. I recognized the pain because I had been there. I had lived with that same struggle, the weight of putting on a strong face, pretending everything was fine, while battling my own demons inside. This wasn't just a gut feeling. It's backed by data that reveals just how many people, especially in the Black community, are silently struggling too.

- One in five adults in the U.S. experiences mental illness each year (National Institute of Mental Health, 2023).
- Black Americans are more likely to experience persistent symptoms of emotional distress and are less likely to receive mental health treatment compared to white Americans. (American Psychiatric Association, 2022).
- Nearly half of college students report moderate to serious psychological distress, including anxiety and depression, affecting their daily functioning. (American College Health Association, 2023).

But numbers don't tell the whole story. Behind each statistic is a life (a student, a brother, a mentor) fighting to stay afloat.

The Weight of Silence and Denial

For far too long, I kept my struggles with mental health to myself. I convinced myself I was fine, that I didn't need help, that I could pray my way through it. But deep down, I knew I wasn't okay. It wasn't until a major turning point that I truly started to face the reality of my mental health.

When I began seeing a therapist regularly, things started to change. I also started meeting with a psychiatrist every three months. Initially, I was hesitant. The stigma surrounding mental health, especially within my community, had kept me in denial for so long. I'd tell myself that I could manage on my own. But when I finally admitted that I needed help, I took the first step toward healing.

Opening Up: The Strength in Vulnerability

It wasn't easy to be open about my struggles, but therapy gave me the space to do so. I learned coping strategies, like deep breathing techniques to calm my anxiety. I started journaling, which eventually led to the creation of my #WalkingMinistry and Inspire Me Moment videos. Through these channels, I not only found an outlet for my emotions but also began to help others who were struggling with the same things.

Through therapy, I also discovered the importance that medication is a tool to support you. At first, I resisted it. I didn't want to rely on pills to manage my emotions. But with guidance from my psychiatrist, I learned to embrace the medication, which helped me find a balance I had been desperately searching for. Now, I call them my "happy pills," and I make sure I never miss a dose.

But even with therapy and medication, what sustained me most was the sense of connection through community and through my faith.

The Healing Power of Community and Faith

One of the most significant aspects of my healing journey has been the role of community and faith. Once I started sharing about my struggles, I realized I wasn't alone. There are so many people who are going through similar challenges, and they need to know that they're not alone either.

Connecting with others who have shared experiences has been incredibly empowering. I've found a deeper connection with my community when I started talking. And my faith, which was always important to me, has grown stronger as I've learned to rely on it as a source of strength and comfort.

Faith has provided me with peace, but I've also learned that faith doesn't mean you don't need support. I can't just pray, and hope things will get better without taking active steps toward healing. The journey involves being open to therapy, medication (if needed), and support from those around you. Together, these elements create a holistic approach to healing, one that doesn't leave you feeling like you're carrying the weight alone.

Mental Health in the Black Community

Even now, mental health is still taboo in many communities of color. We will talk about diabetes or high blood pressure, but mention anxiety or depression, and some spaces, the room gets quiet.

Too many people are suffering in silence. The kind of silence that kills dreams, drowns out prayers, and keeps people from healing. We're often told to "man up" or "just pray about it"—and while faith is essential, therapy and mental health care are also tools God can use.

According to the National Alliance on Mental Illness (n.d.), nearly two-thirds of people with mental illness don't receive treatment, and that stigma is still one of the biggest barriers. In our community, silence isn't just cultural—it's generational. We need to change the narrative so that healing becomes normal, not hidden.

Now don't get me wrong – prayer is powerful. But we also have to recognize that therapy and professional support are just as vital. It's time we started treating mental health with the same urgency and care that we give to physical health.

The Ripple Effect: Mental Health's Impact on the Community

The reality is that mental health struggles don't just affect the individual, they change families, communities, and society as a whole. When young people are struggling, it affects their academic performance, their relationships, and their sense of purpose. Charmaine's struggles reminded me of the importance of addressing mental health in schools, at home, and in our communities.

We need to normalize conversations about mental health and make it okay for people to seek help. It's about breaking the silence, offering support, and encouraging others to act. Breaking the stigma starts with one voice, one story, one honest conversation at a time. And if my voice can help someone else find their healing—then it's worth every word.

Final Thought: Walking Through the Darkness

Are you checking in on your mental health the same way you check your physical health?

_____

_____

_____

_____

If someone in your life is struggling, have you created a space where they feel safe to talk?

_____

_____

_____

What step can you take today to normalize conversations around mental health?

_____

_____

_____

_____

You don't have to carry it alone. Help is out there. Let's walk through it together.

Inspire Me Moment:
Put Your Faith to Work

Faith is not just about believing—it's about taking action. True healing and growth require steps forward, even when the path isn't clear. As you reflect on what it means to walk in faith, ask yourself: Are you putting your faith to work?

"Put some feet on your faith and watch dreams turn into footsteps on the path to success."

Reflection:
Faith isn't just about believing—it's about doing. A dream without action is just a wish, and faith without movement is like a car without fuel—it won't take you anywhere. Every step forward brings your vision to life, turning what once seemed impossible into reality.

Move with purpose, trust the process, and take the next step—even when you can't see the full road ahead. Faith works best when it's in motion.

Final Thought:
It's not enough to hope—**put your faith in motion and let your steps create the path to your success.**

Live Out Loud Challenge:
Put Your Faith to Work

Faith isn't passive, it's active. This challenge invites you to reflect on how belief becomes a bold movement, and how trust transforms into tangible change.

Connect

Reach out to someone whose faith helped them navigate uncertainty. Ask: *"What gave you the courage to take that leap? How did your faith move from belief to action?"*

Reflect

With a trusted peer, revisit a time when faith pushed you beyond fear—when logic said "stop," but something deeper said "go." What did you learn about yourself? About the nature of trust?

Support

Encourage a younger person to see faith not just as hope—but as a series of bold steps. Share a story about moving forward, even without all the answers, opened the door to something greater.

Wellness Check-In
Mental Health is Real

Purpose: This check-in invites you to pause, feel what's real, and care for your mental health with compassion. Healing is ongoing—it's a rhythm of awareness, release, and renewal.

The Check-In Circle
Pause

> Take three deep breaths. Inhale slowly. Exhale fully. Be here, now.

Acknowledge

> Ask yourself: "How am I really feeling?"
> Choose three words to name your emotions. Write them down or say them aloud.

Release

> If any feelings feel heavy, name them—and imagine setting them down. Say: "I don't have to carry this alone."

Affirm

> Speak this over yourself: *"My mental health matters. I honor my emotions and seek peace daily."*

Rebuild

> List one thing you'll do this week to support your mental well-being—call someone, move your body, write it out.

Final Word

Mental health care isn't extra, it's essential. Be still. Be kind to yourself. And know that seeking help is strength, not shame.

The Inner Circle Club

**You've just stepped through something powerful.
Now it's time to speak on it and allow your "NET" Work!**

This is your space to connect, reflect, and build community with other readers.

CHAPTER 6: What Forgiveness Frees

- What has forgiveness set you free from?

- Is there someone you've needed to forgive—even if they never asked?

- What does freedom feel like after the release?

Start your day with clarity. What are you feeling this morning? What do you need more of—peace, purpose, joy? Use this space to check in with your heart before the world rushes in.

Morning Journal

(Remember)

IMMERSE YOURSELF IN THE PRACTICE OF A FOCUSED MORNING JOURNAL—A POWERFUL TOOL THAT CAN POSITIVELY SHAPE YOUR MINDSET AND WELL-BEING.

(Day):	*(Month):*	*(Year):*

Today's Affirmation

Goal of the day

(To Do) Priority of the day:

○ _____
○ _____
○ _____

(Thoughts)

SET INTENTIONS FOR CLARITY, VITALITY, AND INNER PEACE, AND FEEL THE POSITIVE IMPACT THROUGHOUT THE DAY.

(Morning Rituals Checklist)

ROADMAP TO AN ENERGIZED AND PURPOSEFUL START.

MEDITATE ○   ○ MAKE BED

JOURNAL ○   ○ READ

SELF CARE ○   ○ MOVEMENT

◉ TO START   ⊘ OK   ⊖ DELAY   ⊘ STUCK   ⊗ CANCEL

CHAPTER 7:
THE POWER OF BROTHERHOOD

Opening Reflection

Picture this: You're standing at the starting line of a long, winding journey. The road ahead is unfamiliar, filled with unseen twists and hills you can't imagine yet. You lace up your shoes, take a deep breath—and start walking.

At first, it feels manageable. You tell yourself, *"I've got this."* Step by step, you push forward. But soon, the weight of it all creeps in the fatigue, the doubts, the moments when every stride feels heavier than the last.

Just when you're ready to collapse, you hear it: footsteps. Not yours—someone else's. You look around, and there they are. A mentor offering wisdom from battles you haven't yet fought. A peer matching your pace, challenging you to keep going. A younger traveler looking up to you, reminding you that you're not just walking for yourself—you're blazing a trail for someone else. That's when you realize: you were never meant to walk this road alone.

This chapter is a reminder that strength isn't just built in solitude—it's forged in connection. It's about the people who guide you, walk with you, and inspire you to become who you were always meant to be.

Because in the end, life's greatest journeys aren't about how far you can go by yourself, they're about who you bring along for the walk. That realization shifted something in me. It made me think about the relationships that shaped my own path and how none of my growth happened in isolation.

The Power of Connections

No One Succeeds Alone

Throughout life, we all need guidance, encouragement, and accountability to navigate challenges, seize opportunities, and step fully into our purpose.

As it has been said countless times, people come into our lives for a reason, some for a season, and others for a lifetime. Regardless of who we are or where we come from, one truth remains the same: **We don't succeed alone.** And each interaction has its place in your life.

Whether you're a brother, sister, leader, student, parent, friend, or dreamer, **the quality of your relationships often determines the quality of your journey.**

The key is learning to build with the right people—and knowing why their presence matters. That's where purposeful relationships come in. And over the years, I've come to believe that every person needs a certain circle of people who reflect where you have been, where you are, and where you are going.

The People You Need in Your Life

A while back, I heard a Men's Day church sermon that described the three types of men every man need in their life:

1. **A Mentor (Paul)** – Someone who guides you, pours into you, and provides wisdom.

2. **A Peer (Barnabas)** – A trusted friend or brother who walks the journey alongside you.

3. **A Mentee (Timothy)** – Someone you pour into, uplift, and help grow.

My strongest moments—professionally, personally, and spiritually—were when I had all three of these relationships active and thriving. These connections shaped real moments, real growth, and real transformation. A 2018 survey conducted by the Movember Foundation found that nearly one in three men say they have no close friends they can confide in. That's why real brotherhood isn't just helpful—it's life-giving.

> *"As iron sharpens iron, so one person sharpens another."* —
Proverbs 27:17

That's what brotherhood does—it doesn't just walk with you. It *refines* you. It's where transformation begins. Because brotherhood sharpens, challenges, and sustains us when the world tells us to stand alone. Let me share a story about how this really hit home for me.

Purposeful Relationships

One morning, I was out walking the track between John Hay and Cleveland School of the Arts, part of my Walking Ministry routine. I kept thinking about the students I work with, particularly those who struggle with networking and relationship-building. They often don't understand how valuable relationships can be in opening doors, shaping opportunities, and helping them grow.

Just the day before, I was in a meeting with some students, and one of them made a comment that stuck with me. It wasn't intentionally rude, but it lacked awareness. I thought, *if only they understood the way they speak, the way they interact with people, especially people who might help them in the future.* That moment made me reflect on my own journey – the relationships that changed my life and the people who showed up at the right time, for the right reason.

As I continued walking, I thought about the three kinds of relationships that we all need, and I've been blessed to experience them in my life:

1. The Mentor – Someone Who Guides You

I think about the mentors who saw my potential, even when I didn't. They weren't perfect, but they gave counsel, wisdom, and direction. Just like Paul had Barnabas, I had people who guided me when the path was unclear.

Who is pouring into you?

Some of my most impactful mentors include:

- My father, Sumlor Harris, Sr., who, despite our growing pains, taught me perseverance, resilience, and integrity.
- My godfather, the late Rev. George Q. Brown, then Pastor of

Second New Hope Missionary Baptist Church, who nurtured my faith.

- My academic advisor, Dr. Johnson O. Akinleye, at Bethune-Cookman College (now University), who later became the 12th Chancellor of North Carolina Central University. His academic and leadership guidance shaped my path.

2. The Peer – Someone Who Walks with You

Then there are those peers—your brothers in the trenches. The people you build with, struggle with, and celebrate wins alongside. Paul had Silas. We all need that one friend who *gets it.*

Who is walking beside you?

My peers have been essential to my journey, at various points in my life:

- Brian, who I met in grade school through high school, always pushing me to grow.
- Robert, who helped me see the world differently during college.
- Cliff, a lifelong friend through my 20s and 30s, holding me accountable through life's highs and lows.
- And other brothers, including those from my fraternity and lodge, who help keep me grounded.

3. The Mentee – Someone You Pour Into

Then there are mentees—young men looking up to us, often

without us even realizing. Paul mentored Timothy. We too have a responsibility to pour into the next generation.

Who is learning from you?

My first Timothy is my son, Anthony II. Through him, I've learned the weight and joy of guiding the next generation. And to every young man I encounter—through work, ministry, or community engagement—my mission remains: *to instill a desire for growth by living an exemplary life as an effective and exceptional father, friend, educator, leader, artist, and supporter to those that shall cross my path.*

I must also acknowledge my brother and fellow educator, Odell Brown. Odell started as a Timothy—young, enthusiastic, and committed to leading scholars. Over the years, our bond shifted from mentor-mentee to genuine friendship. Today, I consider him a Barnabas in my life. Watching him grow as a leader, and now as a father to his first-born son, has been an honor. He's inspiring others—just as he's inspired me.

These relationships—across generations—remind me that legacy isn't built alone. It's built through intentional investment in others.

Building Community through Courageous Connections

As you reflect on the principles of connection, reflection, and support, remember these aren't just ideas, they're invitations to live more intentionally. They call each of us to build relationships that are rooted in purpose, authenticity, and courage.

Connect: Who in your life can you reach out to today? Connection starts with you. Whether it's a text, a phone call, a note of encouragement, or simply showing up, take the initiative to nurture your community.

Reflect: Pause and evaluate the relationships shaping your journey. Are they helping you grow? Are you showing up as the kind of friend, mentor, partner, or guide that you needed yourself? Reflection is a catalyst for becoming better—for us and for those we walk with.

Support: Living out loud isn't just about what we gain, it's about what we give. How can you support someone else today? Whether it's through listening, encouraging, or offering a helping hand, your investment in others is part of your legacy.

Building a strong community starts with you. One that empowers us to live with purpose, growth, and service. And the journey of connections is never easy, but it's always worth it.

Final Thought: Building Courageous Connections

Let's make the commitment to connect, reflect, and support the people who matter most. If these people don't exist in your life, it's time to start building those relationships today.

Who is your Paul? Who pours wisdom into you, challenges you to grow, and sees your potential even when you can't? *Write their name (and why) or commit to finding them.*

_____

_____

_____

Who is your Barnabas? Who walks beside you, shoulder to shoulder, as you grow, strive, and stand in the fight together? *Write their name (and why) or commit to seeking that partnership.*

_____

_____

_____

Who is your Timothy? Who is looking up to you, waiting for you to notice, guide, and lift them into their own greatness? *Write their name (and why) or commit to pouring into someone new.*

_____

_____

_____

Success is not a solo journey; it's one we take together.

Inspire Me Moment: Becoming

As we walk through life, we often look back and wonder if we are becoming the person we once needed. The journey to living out loud isn't just about embracing who we are, it's about growing into the version of ourselves that our younger selves would be proud of. Before you move forward, take a moment to reflect on your own journey of becoming.

> *"Become the person your younger self would want to look up to."*
>
> *Goitsemang Mvula*

Reflection:

Who did you look up to as a child? Was it someone strong, wise, kind, or resilient? Now, ask yourself, are you becoming that person? Every decision you make, every lesson you learn, and every challenge you overcome is shaping you into the role model your younger self once needed. But becoming that person doesn't happen by chance, it requires **intentional growth, self-awareness, and a commitment to progress.**

Final Thought:

Your journey isn't just about you. It's about **becoming your best self is a lifelong commitment to growth, reflection, and leaving behind a legacy of inspiration.**

Live Out Loud Challenge: Becoming

Growth is a lifelong journey of reflection, connection, and bold intention. This challenge invites you to honor your past, engage with your present, and invest in the future you're building.

Connect

Have a conversation with an elder, mentor, or someone you admire about the lessons they've gained through life's highs and lows. Ask them: *"What experiences most shaped your growth—and how would you guide someone walking a similar path today?"*

Reflect

With a trusted friend or peer, explore this question: *"What would our younger selves think of who we are today?"* Are you aligned with your deeper purpose? What needs to shift so you can live more fully into your potential?

Support

Help someone newer on the journey—whether younger or simply earlier in their evolution—articulate a bold, authentic goal. Encourage them to take one small but intentional step toward it today. Growth isn't just personal; it's generational.

Wellness Check-In
Never Walk Alone

Purpose: This check-in centers your circle. Real growth happens in relationships; those who guide us, walk beside us, and look up to us. Take a moment to reflect, reconnect, and re-engage.

The Check-In Circle

Pause

Close your eyes. Take three deep breaths. As you exhale, picture the people who've shaped you—mentors, brothers, sons, friends.

Reflect

Think about your circle. Which connection needs more care right now? How can you be more present, consistent, or encouraging in that relationship?

Affirm

Say aloud or write down:

"I don't walk alone. I'm connected to purpose-filled people who grow with me and push me to be better."

Rebuild

Choose one action this week to strengthen one of those connections—call, check in, or simply show up with love.

Final Word

Brotherhood is built, not stumbled into. Walk with intention, and you'll never walk alone.

The Inner Circle Club

**You've just stepped through something powerful.
Now it's time to speak on it and allow your "NET" Work!**

This is your space to connect, reflect, and build community with other readers.

CHAPTER 7: The Power of Brotherhood

- Who are your brothers in the struggle and in the rise?

- What makes a bond feel safe, sacred, and strong?

- What's one way you've been a brother to someone else?

Your dreams are seeds of possibility. Use this space to capture the visions, goals, or moments that keep calling you forward—no matter how bold.

Dream Journal

(Remember)

EMBARK ON A SACRED JOURNEY WITHIN THROUGH DAILY DREAM JOURNALING—A SPIRITUAL PRACTICE THAT UPLIFTS YOUR MINDSET AND NURTURES WELL-BEING.

(Day):   *(Month):*   *(Year):*

(Dream Overview)   RECORD A DETAILED DESCRIPTION OF THE DREAM. INCLUDE PEOPLE, PLACES, EMOTIONS, AND ANY VIVID DETAILS.

Mood Tracker	○ ○ ○ ○ ○	*(People and Relationships)*
Lucidity Level	○ ○ ○ ○ ○	
Sleep Quality	○ ○ ○ ○ ○	
Recurring?	YES ○ NO ○	
Interrupted?	YES ○ NO ○	

(Emotions Felt) NOTE THE EMOTIONS EXPERIENCED DURING THE DREAM. HOW DID THE DREAM MAKE YOU FEEL?

(Interpretation) DIVE DEEP INTO DREAM INTERPRETATION — DECODE MESSAGES, SYMBOLS, AND INSIGHTS

CHAPTER 8:
WALKING IN YOUR PURPOSE

Opening Reflection

Imagine standing at a crossroads where history whispers through the trees, and the future hums quietly beneath your feet. That's what New Orleans felt like.

This wasn't just another trip. It was a pilgrimage—through legacy, leadership, and the sacred ground of those who walked before me. Every oak tree at Dillard, every brick at Xavier, every student striving at Southern spoke a truth louder than any sermon: Purpose doesn't just call you. It demands a response.

Faith was no longer just a belief. It had to become motion. Having vision only wasn't enough, it needed mission. Dreams couldn't stay on the page—they needed footprints behind them.

Between campus walks, community service, late-night beignets, and a sermon that hit like lightning, I realized something: the journey isn't just about moving forward. It's about moving with intention. Every step matters. Every detour teaches. Every moment demands faith in action.

This chapter isn't just about chasing dreams. It's about walking them out – one faithful, sometimes uncertain, but always courageous – step at a time. That spiritual charge I felt in New Orleans didn't stay confined to emotion; it moved me toward action. As I set foot on these campuses, I wasn't just taking a trip. I was walking into a deeper understanding of how vision turns into a mission.

Vision-Mission Quest

A Journey Through Purpose

New Orleans has a way of making you reflect on the past while simultaneously pushing you toward the future. Maybe it's the soulful energy of the city, or the rich history of resilience and faith woven into every street. This time, my visit wasn't just about sightseeing, it was about walking with purpose, embracing faith in motion, and understanding that mission work makes the vision work.

Campus Visits: Legacy in Motion

Walking through Dillard University, I felt an unshakable sense of purpose—like I was stepping into the very dreams of those who came before me. The Avenue of the Oaks stood as a symbol of endurance, much like the institution itself. Dillard, founded in 1869, has long upheld its mission to produce ethical, knowledgeable, and socially responsible graduates. Even after storms and hardships, it remains a pillar of resilience.

At Xavier University of Louisiana, the only historically Black Catholic university in the U.S., I saw a different kind of legacy – one built on faith, service, and academic excellence. Xavier has launched countless Black professionals in medicine and pharmacy, and its mission of service is woven into the fabric of its existence.

Southern University, with its flagship campus in Baton Rouge, is the only HBCU system in the nation, expanding opportunities for Black students across multiple institutions. Public service, innovation, and excellence define its culture, preparing students to lead and uplift their communities.

Each institution reminded me that HBCUs exists because someone had a vision and put in the mission work to make it real.

It is always refreshing to speak with scholars about their HBCU experience. Todd Welch, Mr. Dillard University, spoke highly of the academic rigor and commitment to growth at Dillard. His pride in representing a jewel of the South was clear.

At Xavier, something caught my attention, the absence of a designated Greek plot area. For many HBCUs, these spaces symbolize history, identity, and community. It made me reflect on the importance of expansion, not just tradition. Are we making room for growth, or are we limiting our vision?

After witnessing the legacy of purpose across those campuses, I needed to sit with the deeper meaning of what it meant to walk with intention. That reflection led me to the City of Love Church, where a new kind of lesson awaited. One not taught in lecture halls but preached from the pulpit.

Faith in Action: The City of Love Experience

One of the most powerful moments of this journey came at City of Love Church. Bishop Lester Love didn't just preach; he ignited a call to action. He spoke about faith in motion, explaining that believing in something without taking steps toward it is like having a map but never walking the path.

One line that struck me was:

"God can't bless what you won't move toward."

That hit differently. How many times do we pray for change but stay in the same place? How often do we say we want something but never take the first step?

That's when it clicked—this Walking Ministry is more than a hashtag. It's a metaphor for life. Faith without work is dead, and a vision without mission is nothing more than a passing thought.

Inspired by the sermon's charge to put faith into motion, I didn't want to just *hear* the word, I wanted to *live* it. That opportunity came through serving alongside students determined to conduct that mission in real-time.

Community Service: Collective Impact

During my time in New Orleans, I had the privilege of serving alongside students from Dillard, Xavier, and SUNO. It reminded me that mission work isn't just an individual task, it's a collective effort. These students weren't just checking off service hours; they were strengthening their communities and continuing the legacy of those before them.

> ➤ **Vision isn't just personal, it's communal.**

If we don't contribute to the next generation, how can we expect the work to continue? Giving back isn't just a choice, it's a responsibility.

After a day filled with mission and movement, the quiet of the evening offered something different, a chance to sit, reflect, and absorb the sacred stillness that often reveals purpose in the most unexpected ways.

Finding Purpose in Unexpected Places

Later that evening, Carlie, Nicholas, and I sat at Café Du Monde, indulging in New Orleans' most famous beignets. What was supposed to be a casual snack turned into a moment of deep reflection.

Between laughter and the powdered sugar on my fingertips, it hit me. God's plan for us is already written, but it's up to us to read the script and follow through. Sometimes, the most profound reflections happen in the most unexpected places. New Orleans had given me more than just sights and sounds, it had given me clarity.

The journey isn't just about walking; it's about pausing long enough to take in the lessons along the way. New Orleans didn't just teach me, it reminded me. Purpose walks with you. Vision requires your steps. And faith? Faith moves.

Final Thought: Your Mission Work Makes Vision Work

As I wrapped up my time in New Orleans, I kept coming back to the balance between vision and mission.
It's not enough to see where you want to go; you must be willing to put in the work to get there.

So now, I ask you:
What vision has been placed on your heart, but remains untouched because you haven't stepped into action?

_____

_____

_____

Where in your life are you maintaining instead of expanding?

_____

_____

_____

What first step can you take today to move from dreaming to doing?

_____

_____

_____

_____

So, what's your mission work?

Inspire Me Moment:
Happy New You!

Stepping into purpose requires renewal—a commitment to growth, transformation, and becoming the best version of yourself. This isn't just about a new year, it's about a new mindset, a new approach, and a new you. So, what will you do with this opportunity?

"Happy new dreams. Happy new days. Happy new desires. Happy new ways. Happy New Year. Happy New You."

Reflection:
No matter how the past year unfolded—good, bad, or indifferent—you made it. **You survived. You endured. And that alone is worth celebrating.** But survival isn't the goal, thriving is.

With every new year, new day, and new moment, you can step forward, embrace change, and create something new. **Transformation isn't about waiting for the perfect moment. It starts with one decision, one step, one bold move.**

So, this year, let's stop making empty resolutions and start making intentional plans. **This isn't just about wishing for change, it's about committing to the work it takes to grow.**

Final Thought:
This is more than just a new year, it's a **new chance to rise, grow, and step boldly into your next chapter. Welcome to a Happy New You!**

Live Out Loud Challenge: Happy New You!

Growth doesn't wait for January 1st. Every day holds the power to declare a new season—with bold vision, clear action, and community.

Connect
Reach out to someone who made a courageous shift in their life—whether it was changing careers, improving their health, healing relationships, or pursuing a purpose-driven dream. Ask: **What sparked your change and how did you stay committed when times became difficult?**

Reflect
Partner with a peer to create a vision board or draft an action plan. What bold moves are you ready to make this year? How can you hold each other accountable when motivation fades?

Support
Challenge a younger person or someone newer on the journey to turn their vision into action. Don't just talk about dreams, *help them take the first step today.* Break it down into one doable move they can complete within the next 24 hours. **Because momentum isn't magic—it's made.**

Wellness Check-In
Walking in Your Purpose

Purpose: This check-in helps you clarify your purpose, align with your mission, and take real steps toward fulfilling your calling—with faith, strategy, and intention.

3 Actions

1. **Define Your Mission.** Write a one-sentence mission statement. Then list 3 clear steps to bring it to life.

2. **Move with Intention.** Go for a short walk. With each step, repeat: *"I am walking toward my vision."*

   Visualize yourself overcoming any obstacle that tries to block your path.

3. **Affirm Your Calling.** Say aloud: *"I am walking boldly in my purpose. Every step I take is guided by faith and vision."*

   Optional: Speak or write a prayer to stay grounded in your mission.

2 Reflection Prompts

- What's one calling that has been tugging at your heart—and what's held you back?

- What small, intentional step can you take this week to honor that calling?

1 Final Word

Purpose isn't passive, it requires motion. Start walking. Your vision will meet you on the path.

The Inner Circle Club

**You've just stepped through something powerful.
Now it's time to speak on it and allow your "NET" Work!**

This is your space to connect, reflect, and build community with other readers.

CHAPTER 8: Walking in Your Purpose

- What's your mission—not just your dream?

- When did faith move from belief to action for you?

- What "footprints" are you leaving behind for others?

Your healing is a priority—not a luxury. What's one way you'll take care of yourself today? Use this space to design your rest, your boundaries, and your joy.

Self-Care *Journal*

DATE: / /

S   M   T   W   T   F   S

How am I feeling today?

Mental	Physical	Spiritual

Today I'm Grateful for

Today I'm Grateful for

Water Intake

1   2   3   4   5   6   7   8   (Glass)

Mood of the Day

Notes/Reminder

For Tomorrow

PART III:
BUILDING BEYOND

Theme: Purpose, legacy, leadership, and service

"When you build with heart, what you create lasts beyond your lifetime."

This section is about stepping fully into purpose by taking what you've learned and using it to lift others, leave impact, and live out loud.

You are the author of your reality. What are you calling into your life? Be bold. Be specific. Write out the visions, actions, and affirmations that align with the life you deserve.

MANIFESTATION PLANNER

DATE: S   M   T   W   T   F   S

VISUALIZATION

I WANT
TO MANIFEST

I SEE

_____

_____

I HAVE

_____

_____

I FEEL

_____

_____

LIMITING BELIEFS I NEED GET RID OF

TO-DO LIST

○

○

○

○

○

○

○

MY DAILY AFIRMATION

ACTION PLAN

MY PRAYER TO THE UNIVERSE

CHAPTER 9:
LEGACY IN ACTION

Opening Reflection

Every door you walk through, every chance you're given, every hand that pulls you up didn't happen by accident. Someone built that bridge. Someone sacrificed. Someone believed in a future they might never see but planted seeds anyway.

Giving back isn't just charity. It's love in motion. It's the invisible echo of gratitude that moves from generation to generation. When we give, we don't just hand over time or money—we hand over hope. We tell someone else,

"You matter. Your dreams matter. Your future matters."

In this chapter, you'll step into the journey of building bridges for others the same way others once built them for you. You'll meet the mentors, the organizations, and the moments that shaped a life and you'll be challenged to ask yourself:

- Whose future are you investing in today?

Because true greatness isn't measured by what you achieve. It's measured by what you pass on. That belief—that legacy is built through intentional love and service—has shaped every step of my journey. And it begins with a choice: to give back in ways that matter.

Love in Motion: Giving Back

Investing in the Next Generation

Giving back is more than just an act—it's a responsibility. The opportunities we have, the doors that open for us, the hands that reach out to pull us forward—none of them happens in isolation. We rise because someone before us paved the way. And when we have the chance, we must do the same for those coming behind us.

As *"bell hooks"* (2000) reminds us, "Love is an action, never simply a feeling." That quote hits differently when you consider what giving back really means. For me, investing in others—whether through mentoring, scholarships, or showing up—is love in motion. It's how I pour into others the same way I was once poured into. This work is about legacy, yes, but it's also about love.

Two organizations have played a major role in shaping my journey—Youth Opportunities Unlimited (Y.O.U.) and the United Negro College Fund (UNCF). Their missions are different, but their purpose is the same: ensuring that young people are prepared for success.

My commitment to give back found its earliest roots in the spaces where I worked directly with young people. One of the most formative experiences came through an organization that always felt like home.

Walking into Legacy

I was on my way to an event hosted by **Youth Opportunities Unlimited** (Y.O.U.), an organization dedicated to helping students gain workforce readiness skills. Y.O.U. wasn't just another program to me—it was one of the first jobs where I truly felt at home. I worked as a Career Specialist, helping students develop the skills they needed to step confidently into the workforce. This was one of the only jobs I've had where, during my exit interview, I told them,

"If you ever need me, call me."

And they did – every single year. I've continued to come back to support the Youth Career Olympics, a powerful event that gives students the opportunity to sharpen their job readiness skills through firsthand activities.

Walking into that event was like stepping back into my past. I saw students who reminded me of the young men and women I had once helped. I saw mentors who had poured into me years ago. And I saw a cycle, a beautiful-powerful cycle of people investing in the next generation.

The Youth Career Olympics event is filled with young people learning everything from resume writing to networking to nailing job interviews. It was more than just a workshop—it was preparation for life. This is what success looks like investing in the next generation, ensuring they have the tools to succeed before they even step into the workforce.

During my time as a Career Specialist, I had one student who stood out, Latia Mays. She took part in the public speaking category, and while I can't recall if she officially placed first, I remember the pride she had in preparing for the competition. She was the little engine that could—determined, focused, and unwilling to let anything deter her. In my eyes, she is always a winner. Her drive and commitment were a reminder that when young people are given opportunities, they will rise to the occasion.

Another defining moment came when I reconnected with Channon Cotton, a former student who later became mentor. Watching her work with students on their college essays and job applications was a beautiful moment. To see her paying it forward with the guidance she once received. It was a full-circle moment, one that reaffirmed why I continue to pour into young people.

While Y.O.U. gave me the chance to invest in students locally, UNCF connected me with a national movement. One that is rooted in history, legacy, and the power of collective impact. UNCF is a name synonymous with educational access and Black excellence. For over 80 years, this organization has opened doors, removed barriers, and invested in the futures of over 500,000 Black students across the nation.

The **United Negro College Fund (UNCF)** expanded my purpose nationally linking me to a greater collective mission for educational equity and access.

UNCF: The Power of Collective Investment

UNCF was founded in 1944 by Dr. Frederick D. Patterson, then president of Tuskegee Institute, alongside legendary educator and activist Dr. Mary McLeod Bethune of Bethune-Cookman. Their vision was simple yet revolutionary—to unite historically Black colleges and universities (HBCUs) under a single fundraising effort, ensuring that students had access to higher education regardless of financial barriers. They knew that collective power was stronger than individual efforts, and their leadership laid the foundation for what would become one of the most influential scholarship organizations in history.

But my connection to UNCF didn't start with board meetings or leadership roles—it began much earlier, in a living room with a remote, a telephone, and a young boy who simply wanted to have influence.

A Spark of Generosity: My Philanthropic Pursuits

One of the most significant milestones in UNCF's history was the Lou Rawls Parade of Stars Telethon. This was a televised fundraising event that, over the years, raised hundreds of millions of dollars for HBCU scholarships. From the late 1970s through the early 2000s, this annual event featured some of the biggest names in entertainment, all coming together to support Black students and their futures.

I remember watching the Lou Rawls Parade of Stars as a child, mesmerized by the performances and the stories of students whose lives were changed by UNCF scholarships. But there was one moment that truly shaped me when I saw my father on TV, presenting a $5,000 donation. Seeing him contribute to a cause so much bigger than himself left a lasting impression on me.

Inspired, I turned to my mother and asked her to call in and donate on my behalf. I had no idea how powerful that $7 would become—

not in money, but in meaning. I just wanted to be part of something bigger. That night, seeing my name scroll across the screen changed me. It wasn't just a donation. It was identity. Purpose. My first taste of what it meant to give back. I wanted to be part of that movement even if it was just a small amount from my allowance.

Imagine the thrill when I saw my name scrolling across the television screen, listing my $7.00 donation. At 10 years old, I had no real understanding of who the founders were, what UNCF truly represented, or even what a Historically Black College and University was. Yet, I gave because I saw my father give. So, I figured if he could invest, so could I.

I didn't realize it then, but that was the beginning of my own journey in philanthropy and advocacy for education. That spark of generosity stayed with me, growing stronger over time. Years later, I would find myself not just donating but leading efforts to raise funds and awareness for UNCF. I had the pleasure of serve as the Founding President of the Northern Ohio Inter-Alumni Council of UNCF and one of the longest serving presidents of the Cleveland Council of Black Colleges Alumni Association. Both opportunities eventually allowed me to serve as the 24th President of the UNCF National Alumni Council.

What began as a childhood moment of inspiration eventually became a lifelong mission—one that carried me from giving seven dollars to sitting among national changemakers.

From Diamond in the Rough to the National Table

As the president, I understood the responsibility of the role, but it wasn't until my first Board of Directors meeting that I fully felt the weight of my position. I found myself seated at a table with the senior leadership of UNCF, board members, and the 37 HBCU college presidents. The moment was surreal. These were the decision-makers shaping the future of HBCUs and here I was, not just in the room, but at the table, adding value and representing thousands of alumni and college students nationwide.

I got choked up for a moment. Here I was, a kid who graduated high school with a 1.906 GPA. A score that most institutions wouldn't have even considered. But HBCUs? They are something different. More specifically, Bethune-Cookman University took a lump of coal like me, molded, shaped, grinded, and polished me until I became that diamond in the rough.

So, there I was at the table with the very leaders who once gave me a chance. From a remedial high student to the National Alumni President—I wasn't just representing myself. I was standing for every student who just needed someone to believe. This wasn't just a full-circle moment. It was proof that when we give back, we give rise.

Final Thought: Investing in the Future is Non-Negotiable

Giving back is more than just financial contributions. It's about **mentorship, time, and creating opportunities for others**. Scholarships and fundraising provide access, but guidance, networking, and advocacy help shape futures just as much. Investing in the next generation is not an option; it's a responsibility.

Who poured into you, and how can you honor their investment by lifting someone else?

_____

_____

_____

What small steps can you take today to support a young person's education or career journey?

_____

_____

_____

In what ways are you leaving a legacy of impact that will open doors for those who come after you?

_____

_____

_____

Legacy isn't just about what you achieve, it's about who you empower along the way.

Full-Circle Moments

From Doubt to the Podium

I stood at the podium, facing a sea of eager graduates—eyes full of hope, hearts racing with uncertainty. They reminded me of myself: I was a kid who I thought was stuck on stupid and parked on dumb, unsure of his next step, standing on the edge of a future I couldn't see yet. That day wasn't just about a speech, it was about passing the torch, healing, and the kind of growth that only comes when you keep walking forward, even when the road feels unclear.

I had been invited to deliver the commencement address, an honor that carried weight beyond words. As I looked at them, I saw reflections of my younger self full of ambition but uncertain of what was to come. I remembered graduating from high school with no clear goal. Sure, I could stay in Cleveland and work in the family business. But was that what I truly wanted? I had applied to several colleges late in the process, leaving me without a clear next move. It felt like I was simply walking on a road to nowhere.

I was scared graduating from high school. Though I may have had a gift for talking, I didn't think I was good enough to do much of anything else. The contrast between then and now was surreal. Imagine, me... a guy who barely graduated high school, now standing in front of students who were about to begin their journey in life. And another thing, would you believe that there were administrators who were against me being the commencement speaker, only to come and congratulate me at the end? Life doesn't just bring things full circle. It brings us back transformed, ready to pour into others what once felt impossible to pour into ourselves.

As I took a deep breath, I knew this was more than just a speech; this was an opportunity to empower into the next generation, to remind them that their walk was just beginning.

What began as a swirl of nerves and reflection quickly transformed into a moment of connection. As I opened my mouth to speak, I realized I wasn't just sharing my story—I was speaking into theirs.

Capturing the Room: More Than a Speech

The excitement in the room was undeniable. Family and friends filled the auditorium, their cheers and applause amplifying the graduates' anticipation. The seniors were anxious, eager, and ready to cross that finish line.

As I started speaking, I caught snippets of conversations and positive affirmations from the crowd. One parent leaned over and said, *"He is preaching now, I hope my son is listening."* That was my sign—I wasn't just giving a speech; I was delivering a message that needed to be heard.

The energy in the room was amazing, but it was the message that mattered most. And so, I began to share the truths I had learned—not just about success, but about survival, struggle, and the winding road of purpose.

The Road Ahead Isn't Straight—But It's Yours

I told them,

> *"You will face many challenges. You will have moments when the road ahead seems uncertain when obstacles appear insurmountable. But remember this: every step, every setback, every victory is part of your story."*

I shared how life had tested me, how my path was anything but straight. There were times when I questioned if I was walking toward purpose or simply wandering. Moments when self-doubt crept in, whispering that I wasn't enough. But through it all, the key wasn't just about moving, it was about moving with intention.

That winding road taught me more than I ever expected. And from it came lessons I now carry everywhere—principles that have grounded my walk and guided my growth.

Lessons from the Walk

As I reflected, I spoke about three things that had kept me going:

1. **Faith in the Process** – Trust that every step has purpose—even the detours. Like sitting in a chair without second-guessing its strength, faith means leaning into the unknown, knowing it's holding you up even when you can't see how.

2. **The Power of Community** – No one walks alone. Your mentors, neighbors, and even strangers can become lifelines. Just like Sesame Street reminds us: "These are the people in your neighborhood. They're the people that you meet when you're walking down the street." Pay attention. Your support system might be closer than you think.

3. **Giving Back Along the Way** – The road isn't yours alone. As you rise, reach back. Share what you've learned. Become the bridge you once needed.

To bring it home, I leaned into a story many of us know, but few of us truly see ourselves in—*The Wiz*. Because sometimes the best lessons come wrapped in melody and metaphor.

Dorothy's Truth: You Had It All Along

Toward the end of my speech, I leaned into a familiar story. I spoke about the journey of Dorothy in *The Wiz* (Lumet, 1978), the soulful adaptation of L. Frank Baum's The Wonderful Wizard of Oz.

"Dorothy spent her entire journey searching for something. Believing that someone else had the key to getting her home,"

I told them. At the beginning of the movie, she doubted herself. Unsure if she was smart enough to teach, capable of showing love, or courageous enough to step outside her comfort zone. She didn't think she had what it took, nor did she realize she possessed everything she needed all along.

In *The Wiz*, Dorothy spends much of her time trying to get back home, only to discover she had the power inside her the whole time. That story reminds me that purpose isn't something you chase—it's something you recognize.

The Scarecrow showed her the brilliance she already had. The Tin Man revealed her ability to love through pain. The Lion reminded her that courage isn't loud, it's steady. They weren't just friends. They were her mirror. And like all of us, she didn't need a wizard. She just needed time, reflection, and a little faith to see herself clearly.

By the time Dorothy and her friends returned to see the Wiz after Eveline's demise, she realized something powerful. I paused, letting the weight of the moment settle in, and then I said,

"She had what she needed all along."

Dorothy had been so focused on finding the next thing that she forgot to celebrate the strength, wisdom, and love she already had.

Dorothy's journey is much like our own. She had to stay on the

Yellow Brick Road, even when she wasn't sure where it would lead. Faith in the process means trusting that every step forward brings you closer to where you're meant to be, even when the path isn't clear. I had to learn that I was trying to get back to a version of me I hadn't yet fully embraced. And when I finally sat with that truth, I realized that I'd had it all along.

She also didn't walk alone. The Scarecrow, Tin Man, and Lion not only needed her encouragement, but also helped her grow in return. That's the power of community—surrounding yourself with people who challenge, uplift, and push you forward when you feel like stopping.

And as Dorothy traveled, she wasn't just receiving help—she was giving it, too. She motivated those around her to believe in themselves, to ease on down the road even when the journey felt tough. Giving back along the way means pouring into others as you move forward, understanding that your journey isn't just for you— but for those coming after you.

Her story reminds us that we don't become powerful by arriving— we discover we've been powerful all along. Like Dorothy, we just need the journey to reveal it.

Dorothy's discovery was a mirror to our own. And as the weight of that realization lingered in the air, I knew it was time to shift the atmosphere—not just with words, but with a sound that would stay with them long after the caps hit the floor.

Ease On Down the Road: A Final Charge

As the room settled after Dorothy's revelation, I took a moment to let the message sink in. Then, the musician that I had planted and cued up, stuck the opening cord and I began to sing "If You Believe" from *The Wiz*. A murmur of surprise rippled through the audience. I even heard that same parent from earlier as she hollered,

> *"Oh, he sings too! Okay!"*

The room shifted and people were engaged, leaning in, nodding their heads. This moment wasn't just about words; it was about connecting with the graduates in a way that stuck.

I reminded them,

> *"You are standing on the shoulders of those who paved the way for you,"*

And understand this, someone is waiting to stand on your shoulders. You are the ancestor someone is praying for. So, walk with courage. Walk with clarity. Walk like your steps are opening doors, not just or you, but for those coming behind you. And trust and believe, they are.

Final Thought: Walking Toward Legacy

The journey of purpose is not about having all the answers. It is about trusting the road ahead, embracing the people you meet along the way, and recognizing the strength you already have. Like Dorothy, you may not always realize that everything you need is already within you.

Where in your life do you need to trust the road, even if you can't see the destination?

_____

_____

_____

Who are the people walking beside you, and how are they helping you grow?

_____

_____

How can you encourage someone else to believe in themselves and keep moving forward?

_____

_____

_____

Your journey is more than a destination; it's a path that shapes those who will walk after you. But through faith, community, and a willingness to give back, you will uncover your true potential.

Inspire Me Moment:
Ease On Down the Road

Purpose isn't about arriving; it's about the journey. The road ahead may have twists and turns, but the key is to keep moving. Walk with confidence, knowing that every step is leading you toward something greater.

"Ease on Down the Road to something better."
From the musical, The Wiz

Reflection:
Life is a journey that is full of twists, turns, and unexpected detours. But no matter how uncertain the road ahead may seem, the key is to **keep moving**.

Just like in *The Wiz*, where Dorothy and her friend's faced challenges but never stopped stepping, you, too, have the power within you to push forward. Each obstacle you face isn't just a roadblock. It's part of your growth to teach life lessons.

There will be setbacks, moments of doubt, and times when the road feels endless. But if you walk with courage, hope, and purpose, you will reach your destination. Some days, it will feel far away. Other days, you'll realize it's closer than you thought.

Final Thought:
No matter how uncertain the path may seem, **ease on down the road with confidence.** Keep stepping, keep believing, and trust that every move forward is shaping you for something greater.

Live Out Loud Challenge:
Ease On Down the Road

The road may twist, stall, or reroute—but the journey still matters. This challenge invites you to walk with purpose, trust your pace, and help someone else step into their next season.

Connect
Talk with someone who's navigated life's unexpected detours. Ask: **"What helped you keep moving forward when the path changed? What wisdom did you pick up along the way?"**

Reflect
With a peer, map out your personal "Life Road Map." Where have you been? What moments built your resilience? What dreams are calling you forward now?

Support
Take a younger person, mentee, or family member on a literal or symbolic walk—through your neighborhood, campus, or just a quiet space. Talk about their journey. Affirm their dreams. Help them name one next step they can take with courage.

Wellness Check-In
The Power of Giving Back

Purpose: Giving back should be meaningful—not draining. This check-in helps you reflect on your legacy, honor your boundaries, and stay energized as you support others.

Today I will stop...

Giving beyond my limits or out of guilt. I will no longer confuse overextending with impact.

Today I will start...

Pouring from a full cup. I'll give intentionally by choosing service that aligns with my values and preserves my peace.

This truth will anchor me...

"I am a vessel of service, giving from a place of abundance, wisdom, and love."

This one action will move me forward...

I'll support one person this week with a simple act—while also protecting space to recharge and reflect.

The Inner Circle Club

You've just stepped through something powerful.
Now it's time to speak on it and allow your "NET" Work!

This is your space to connect, reflect, and build community with other readers.

CHAPTER 9: Legacy in Action

- Who paved the way for you—and how are you returning the favor?

- What kind of legacy are you actively building?

- What's one way you've shown love through service?

There is always something to be thankful for. Even in the tension, there's a truth worth honoring. List what's bringing light to your life, no matter how small.

GRATITUDE JOURNAL

WEEK: _____   MONTH: _____   YEAR: _____

TODAY I'M GRATEFUL FOR

_____

_____

_____

_____

SOMETHING
I'M PROUD OF

WORDS TO INSPIRE THE DAY

TODAY'S AFFIRMATION

_____

_____

_____

TOMORROW I LOOK FORWARD TO

WATER INTAKE

1L   2L   2.5L   3L

HOW HAVE I FELT THIS YEAR?

GOOD   NOT GOOD

CHAPTER 10:
THE POWER OF REFLECTION

Opening Reflection

At first, reflection feels like standing in front of a mirror and facing the person you were, the battles you fought, and the bruises you tried to hide. But if you stay there long enough, something changes. That mirror becomes a window, a view into the life you're still building and the legacy you're still shaping.

This chapter isn't about looking back just to admire or regret. It's about looking back to understand. To honor the people who planted seeds you didn't even know were growing. To realize that every closed door, every hard-earned lesson, and every whispered word of encouragement meant something. By no means were they accidents, instead they were the elements needed for the architecture of your life.

We were never just meant to survive what we went through. We were meant to build with it. Reflection reminds us:

➤ Every mistake you thought would break you became material for your wisdom.

➤ Every teacher, mentor, or friend who believed in you gave you blueprints for becoming.

➤ Every loss, every wrong turn, every doubt weren't detours. They were design elements.

You are standing today because somewhere, someone whispered over you: "Rise anyway."

And now? It's your turn to see yourself not just as a survivor of your past but as a steward of your future.

The reflections staring back at you aren't just memories. They are mirrors that are becoming windows. And through them, you see it clearly now: You were becoming the leader you once needed all along.

As I looked back at the people who shaped me, one name stood out, a quiet force who modeled what leadership could look like long before I had the words to name it.

Legacy Lessons

Becoming the Leader I Once Needed

If I could thank one teacher who left a lasting imprint on my life, it would be Mr. Al Patillo, my fourth-grade teacher and the first Black male educator I ever encountered. As a young Black boy navigating a system that didn't always understand or embrace me, his presence alone shifted the atmosphere. He didn't have to raise his voice to command respect. He didn't have to wear a cape to be a hero. He led with quiet strength and patience, which, looking back, was a radical form of resistance in an environment that often-demanded conformity over compassion.

Seeing someone who looked like me leading with intellect, empathy, and dignity was life-altering. Mr. Patillo didn't just teach curriculum; he modeled presence. He was a mirror, a lighthouse, a seed planter. And unknowingly, he introduced me to the essence of what culturally responsive teaching could look like before I ever knew that term existed.

I remember when I joined the school safety patrol. That orange belt and shiny badge? That was my first taste of leadership. Mr. Patillo took that role seriously. He reminded us that leadership wasn't about a title, it was about how we carried ourselves, even when no one was watching. He'd say,

> *"You represent more than yourself,"*

I still carry those words with me this day.

Years later, I'd discover we were both members of Alpha Phi Alpha Fraternity, Inc. As I came into my own identity as a man and educator, I realized that what he modeled wasn't just good teaching—it was legacy-building. And I'm proud to now carry that torch forward.

The seeds Mr. Patillo planted didn't bloom overnight. But when they did, they pulled me back into the very soil that raised me. But this time, as a teacher.

From Being Taught to Teaching

When I stepped into education, I didn't come with years of intention. I came with lived experience and a calling I hadn't yet named. I returned to Warrensville Heights High School, my alma mater to teach. To work with some of the same teachers who once helped raise me. I was nervous. Humbled. Determined. But the warmth they showed me reminded me that I wasn't just "coming back"—I was stepping into legacy.

Within a few years, I was named Teacher of the Year. I wasn't chasing awards—I was chasing purpose. But that title confirmed the growth that had taken root. Soon after, I was coaching some of those same mentors who once coached me. That's the beauty of education. We don't compete – we contribute. We don't gatekeep – we guide.

But becoming an educator wasn't just about being in front of a classroom. It was about unlearning some things, too, especially the illusion of control.

Learning to Let Go of the Plan

I used to plan perfectly. I had everything mapped out—what students would learn, when they'd learn it, and how they'd perform. Then I looked up one day and realized half the class was failing. That was the lesson.

The issue wasn't the content I was teaching. It was me. I had become rigid and planned for perfection instead of planning for students. I shifted my lens from a teaching-centered to learning-centered perspective. I listened more. I built more room for flexibility, voice, and connection.

When students felt seen, they showed up. When they saw themselves in the learning, they engaged. When they had choices, they took ownership. Once I released the pressure to be less perfect, I created space for real connections. The ones that would ripple far beyond a lesson plan.

Mentoring the Mirror

There is one student that still lives in my heart. I guess you could say he is another Timothy I my life (Chapter 7). At times he was a quiet scholar and gifted artist who didn't believe he belonged in college. In some respects, he was "me" at 18, talented but unsure. I couldn't let him settle for less.

Before graduation, I met with David Davis and his parents to complete the FAFSA together. We sat and applied for several colleges. I reminded him—daily—that his story had value. He eventually enrolled, graduated, and returned to work at the same district. He now mentors' students in the very school where I once taught him. That's the cycle. That's the legacy. That's the work still working.

Every legacy we build begins with a lesson—but it doesn't end there. It extends into how we show up, how we protect others, and how we lead with vision. As I reflected on the educators and mentors who shaped my path, I began to realize that their presence wasn't just formative, it was protective. They saw things in me I hadn't yet seen in myself. They stood guard over my potential.

And so now, let us honor the unseen strength that's carried us. Let us meet the figure who's been here all along… not only watching— but preparing us to accept the mantle ourselves.

You must understand that this was an external transformation for me. But on the inside, I was still wrestling with doubt, with purpose, with worth. And that's when the words found me.

When the Words Find You

Sometimes the weight you carry isn't just from what you've been through. It's from what you've been chosen to carry.

There was a season when I questioned everything. I wasn't the best candidate. I didn't have the cleanest résumé. I had been rejected, overlooked, and in some rooms, flat-out dismissed. But even in silence, the purpose was still speaking.

And then... a word found me. Not in a conference room. Not at a leadership seminar. But in the middle of a church service. God whispered, "You're not broken—you're becoming."

That day, something shifted. Not because a door opened, but because I stopped begging to be let in. You see, I used to think I needed approval to rise. I thought I needed applause to be affirmed. But the oil in your life doesn't require a microphone to be activated. Some of the people who dismissed you didn't realize you were the answer to a prayer they once prayed.

And now, you get to lead with humility, walk with power, and speak to the broken places—because you've lived in them yourself. So yes, I was the student sent to the principal's office for talking too much. But now, I speak life into others and get paid to do so.

I don't just walk into classrooms, I stand in pulpits, boardrooms, and school auditoriums carrying the same message: **you were born with purpose on your breath.** And I don't share to be impressive. I share to remind the wounded, the weary, and the waiting that they still have work to do.

Your *yes* may not come with a title.
It may not trend on social media.
But it might just release somebody else's future.
You don't need permission.
You don't need perfection.
You need power.
And can I tell you what the good news is? You already have it.

So, at time moment, I want you to – Reflect. Reclaim. Rise.
Because this story – your story – isn't finished.
It's just getting started.

Final Thought: Legacy Isn't What We Leave...

Legacy isn't reserved for elders or legends. It's the choices we make today. It's in how we listen, how we lead, and how we lift others when no one's watching.

Who is one person whose legacy has shaped your leadership?

_____

_____

In what ways are you becoming the example you once needed?

_____

_____

_____

What would it look like to carry your influence with both humility and intention?

_____

_____

_____

The most powerful legacy we create isn't found in awards or accolades. It's in the hearts of those we've reached, the lives we've reshaped, and the mirrors we've become.

So, the question isn't just "What are you building?"
The question is: Who are you becoming in the process?

The Watchful Guardian

The Journey with the Guardian Sentinel

The journey through these pages has been one of reflection, transformation, and purpose.

We've walked through stories of resilience, unpacked the weight of our past, and stepped boldly toward a future marked by clarity, connection, and calling.

But woven into every lesson—quietly, faithfully—there has been one presence:

Guardian Sentinel.

He wasn't just introduced in a chapter.

He was never limited to the page.

He showed up in the pauses, in the pivots, in the places where growth began.

He was in the quiet space after each breakthrough, the strength behind each confession, and the echo of every call to rise higher.

He didn't speak loudly—but he always spoke truth.

He didn't rescue you—but he reminded you what you were capable of.

He didn't walk ahead of you—he walked with you.

Because Guardian Sentinel was never a fantasy.

He was a symbol. A spirit. A mirror.

A quiet reminder that we are becoming what we once searched for.

He was watching.

He was waiting.

And through it all—he was walking with you.

But where did he come from?

To understand his purpose, we must begin with his pain.

The Guardian's Journey

Guardian Sentinel wasn't born in glory; he was born in grief.

Not with a cape, but with the weight of invisibility.

His story of origin begins in the shadows of loss, in the ache of injustice, in the quiet sting of being unseen.

But that burden became a spark.

Like so many of us—especially educators, healers, and leaders of color—he didn't rise through privilege. He rose through pain.

His power wasn't handed to him. It was carved by experience.

Each time he was underestimated, overlooked, or misunderstood, something sacred was awakening.

His calling wasn't chosen.

It was revealed.

In the silence after rejection. In the stillness of reflection.

In the whisper that said, "Still, you rise."

The Guardian Sentinel was never perfect. He was willing.

He rose not because he had the answers—but because he refused to let the questions go unanswered.

And as he rose, he was gifted powers—not for show, but for service:

Super strength – the quiet kind, forged by endurance, not applause.

Flight – the inner lift that allowed him to rise above what was meant to hold him down.

Discernment – not gifted from the stars but born through struggle. He could see what others missed because he had lived it.

He didn't just battle injustice—he challenged the voice inside us that said: *This is just the way it is.*

He stood for forgotten neighborhoods.

For overlooked youth.

For stories that deserved to be shouted, not shelved.

But Guardian Sentinel is not a solo act.

He is not here to save us.

He's here to remind us: **we are already becoming.**

He is a symbol.

A standard.

A seed.

And he will walk with us… until we no longer need him because we've become him.

Over time, Guardian Sentinel didn't just walk beside me, he became part of me. And now, if you look closely, you'll see how his powers mirrored your own.

Powers Awakened

You would be surprised to know, the Guardian Sentinel has been seen across every chapter in this book. Sometimes in the shadow, sometimes in spirit, but always there. Not as a savior from above, but as a presence rising within.

- ➢ **When you stepped into brotherhood and built meaningful relationships** – you discovered that no hero rises alone.
- ➢ **When you released the weight of your past** – you tapped into the strength that's been in you all along.
- ➢ **When you rewrote your inner narrative** – you turn silence and shame into sacred testimony.
- ➢ **When you chose peace over anger** – you lifted into freedom and forgave yourself forward.
- ➢ **When you trusted healing even without closure** – you walked with faith, not fear.
- ➢ **When you embraced your mission and moved with purpose** – you aligned your path with divine power.
- ➢ **When you gave back without burning out** – you modeled what it means to lead sustainably and serve joyfully.

- ➤ **When you chose the right builders** – you protected your purpose by building with discernment.

- ➤ **When you empowered others to ask better questions and not just give better answers** – you passed on wisdom, not control. Ownership is when students stop asking for the answers and start asking better questions. That's when you know the learning belongs to them now.

- ➤ **When you reflect on your own becoming** – you realize one light spark many.

- ➤ **When you stepped into the life your younger self needed** – you became the Guardian someone else has been waiting for.

Recognizing your power is one thing.

Walking in it?

That's where true transformation begins.

The Moment of Becoming

You may not wear a cape.

You may not have been endowed with superpowers that were passed down from a glowing rock in the sky.

You were never just stepping into leadership. You were stepping into memory. The child in you needed a hero. Now, others are watching how you become one. Every time you choose integrity over applause, presence over perfection, or people over policy, you embody the Sentinel's spirit.

I got one even better for you. Every time you...

- Step into a room with quiet courage.
- Speak life into someone on the edge.
- Show up when no one else will.
- Challenge the status quo with truth and heart.

...you **are** the Guardian Sentinel.

Your walk may not be on the rooftops or the depths of an ocean. It might be through the school hallways, community meetings, sanctuaries, or the family living rooms.

Whatever space you occupy, you are still guarding something sacred. And the world needs what only you carry.

And just like that, the torch begins to pass.

The Guardian doesn't leave because the work is done.

He steps back... because you're ready.

The Final Watch

Today, we stands bold – not in triumph, but in transition.

The city below is still pulsing with need, still flickering with light and shadow.

But something is different.

There are more lights now.

Not because the fight is over –

But because more Guardians have awakened.

Guardians now exist in classrooms and cafeterias, in community meetings and podcast mics. They may wear hoodies and boots instead of masks and helmets. Instead of referencing comic book characters, they quote positive messages through various social media platforms, music, fashion, or trends. They don't fly above the people – they walk beside them.

With one last glance toward the horizon, he says not goodbye, but something better:

> *"You were never waiting for a hero.*
> *You were becoming one all along."*

And with that, he rises – not to disappear, but to make space for you.

Now it's your turn.

Protect. Build. Believe.

The cape is yours.

Final Thought: The Sentinel Within You

The time for waiting is over—you are ready.
The battles you face are not meant to break you, but to build you.
You have everything you need to rise.

Now the Watch is Yours

You've walked this journey. You've unpacked, reflected, and rebuilt. But this was never just a book. It is a blueprint. And now, the next mission is yours.

ACTIVITY: Design Your Guardian Identity
Who is your Sentinel self?

Take a moment to define your heroic identity—on your own terms.

_____

_____

_____

_____

Name Your Guardian Persona:
Ex: The Quiet Builder. The Legacy Keeper. The Torchbearer.

_____

_____

_____

_____

What Do You Guard?
Your peace? Your family? Your classroom? Your community?

_____

_____

_____

_____

What's Your Superpower?
Resilience? Vision? Emotional intelligence? Creative brilliance?

_____

_____

_____

Your Guardian Mission Statement:
Write 1–2 sentences that declare what your Sentinel self is here to protect, build, or ignite.

_____

_____

_____

Reflection: What Are You Guarding?
What values are you called to stand watch over in this season of your life?

_____

_____

_____

_____

Who are you called to uplift or protect, whether directly or by example?

_____

_____

_____

Where are you being summoned to build, lead, or light the way?

_____

_____

_____

Final Charge:
"The light you carry isn't small. It's sacred."
Protect it. Share it. Build with it.
And most of all—believe in it.

Inspire Me Moment: Long Lasting Impact

True success isn't measured in immediate gains but in the ripples that extend beyond our reach. Giving back means planting seeds that will grow for generations to come.

"Art is made in hindsight."
Virgil Abloh

Reflection:
Sometimes the true value of your actions isn't immediately clear. Even the greatest artists, thinkers, and leaders often don't see the full weight of their impact until years later—or even after they've left this world. The same can be said for us.

Your contributions, big or small, are making ripples that will eventually touch others in ways you can't yet imagine. Whether it's the kindness you show, the lessons you teach, or the way you live your life, everything you do creates a legacy. Even if it feels like no one notices now, trust that your impact is unfolding in someone's life, and it will continue to echo long after you're gone. So, keep creating, keep showing up, and keep sharing your gifts. What you're doing matters.

Final Thought:
Your impact isn't always seen in the moment, but rest assured, every action, every word, every moment you invest in others is creating a legacy that will resonate for generations. Trust that what you do today will create ripples that will continue to ripple long after you're gone.

Live Out Loud Challenge:
Long Lasting Impact

Legacy isn't just what you build, it's what you leave behind. This challenge calls you to honor those who poured into you and to commit to becoming that source of light for someone else.

Connect

Reach out to an elder, mentor, teacher, or guide who helped shape your life. Thank them. Ask: "What kept you going when no one was clapping? How did you stay faithful to the bigger vision?" Let them know: Their impact is still alive in you.

Reflect

With a trusted peer, talk honestly about legacy—not in terms of titles or trophies, but in the quiet daily actions. Ask yourselves: "How do we want to be remembered? What are we truly building today that will outlast us?"

Support

Write a heartfelt letter, note, or voice message to a younger person or someone newer in the journey. Speak life into their future. Remind them: Small steps matter. Faithful work matters. They are already building a legacy.

Wellness Check-In
Reflect. Reframe. Rise.

Purpose: Sometimes we move so quickly that we forget to pause and honor the journey. Reflection is more than memory it's momentum. This check-in is your moment to breathe, to realign with who you've become, and to reclaim the purpose that's been with you all along.

Mind: Guided Self-Reflection – "Looking Inward to Move Forward"

Take a quiet moment to answer these:

- What's one decision from your past that shaped you more than you realized?

- Who was a silent supporter in your journey—someone who saw you when others didn't?

- How has your definition of leadership or success evolved over time?

Now flip the mirror—

- In what ways are *you* now someone else's silent supporter or source of vision?

Body: Grounding Exercise – "Stillness is Strength"

Sit comfortably. Close your eyes. Inhale for 4 counts, hold for 4, exhale for 6.

Repeat for 2–3 minutes.

As you breathe, visualize the roots of a tree beneath you – strong, quiet, steady.

Now say aloud (or in your mind):

"I am rooted in purpose. I am growing in legacy."

Repeat it slowly, 3 times.

Feel your body relax and your mind, realign with who you've become.

Soul: Release & Recommit

Sometimes the hardest work is releasing the old story we've been told about ourselves.

- What belief about yourself are you ready to let go of?
- What is one truth you now claim with confidence?
- Who are you becoming, and what legacy are you ready to leave behind?

Affirmation

"My past taught me. My purpose leads me. I am both the lesson and the legacy."

Say this out loud as a declaration. Write it down and place it somewhere visible this week.

The Inner Circle Club

**You've just stepped through something powerful.
Now it's time to speak on it and allow your "NET" Work!**

This is your space to connect, reflect, and build community with other readers.

CHAPTER 10: The Power of Reflection

- What lessons are you still learning from your past?

- Who helped plant a seed in you—even if it didn't bloom right away?

- What would you tell your younger self about who you've become?

CHAPTER 11:
KEEP WALKING, KEEP BECOMING

Opening Reflection

You made it to this moment.

But the truth is, the journey is just beginning.

This book wasn't just a collection of lessons, it was a mirror, a map, and a reminder that you hold the pen to your own story. Every struggle, every breakthrough, every moment you chose to rise, it's all led you here.

The cape you were searching for –

> It was never hanging in a closet.

> It was always stitched into your spirit.

Now the charge is simple but sacred:

➢ Keep moving forward – even when the steps feel small.

➢ Keep believing – even when growth feels slow.

➢ Keep inspiring – even when no one is clapping.

You are living proof that rejection is redirection. Your testimony declares that your storms didn't stop your destiny. That becoming never ends, it just deepens the experience.

The best chapters of your life aren't behind you.

They're still being written; with every bold step you take.

So, walk with vision.

Walk with heart.

Walk like the world needs what only you carry.

Because it does.

And because you – yes, you – were built for this.

And before you set this book down, I want to let you in on something even deeper.

This wasn't just written *for* you—it was written *with* you in mind.

And maybe even *with* me in mind, too.

The Ongoing Mission

As you reach the last moments of this book, I want to leave you with this final thought: **Your journey has just begun.**

This book has been a reflection and collection of my own struggles, growth, and transformation—but more importantly, it is a testament to the power we all possess to rewrite our story, to embrace the changes we need to make, and to live a life that speaks louder than any fear or regret.

In many ways, writing these pages has been my own therapy. The words, the affirmations, the moments shared are all part of the healing process. **They are not just for you; they are for me, too.** Because we all need reminders that we are enough, that we can change, and that we are worthy of a life lived without hesitation and limits.

If nothing else stays with you, hold on to these truths. Let them echo louder than doubt when the path gets quiet:

- ❖ **You are the author of your own story.** No matter where you start, you have the power to choose how it unfolds.
- ❖ **You can create the life you've always dreamed of.** It won't be easy, but it will be worth it. The road ahead will have its obstacles, but the reward of living out loud, with no regrets, will far exceed any temporary struggle.

❖ **You were never meant to walk this journey alone.** Mentorship and community will always be there, so **lean into them, contribute to them, and build them up for the ones coming behind you.**

I have spent my life striving to lead by example, to not only grow but to inspire growth in others. As I shared before,

> *My mission is to instill a desire for growth by living an exemplary life as an effective and exceptional father, friend, educator, leader, artist, and supporter to those that shall cross my path in life.*

That mission is not just mine. It is an invitation for you to define your own. Understand that my work continues, but yours begins now. Though this book now ends, your journey is wide open.

So now, **it's your turn**. Take everything you've learned, the stories you've read, and the lessons you've absorbed—and apply them. I used to think rejection meant I wasn't enough. But now I understand that sometimes, rejection is just God's redirection. That closed door didn't limit me; it launched me.

Live your life without looking over your shoulder.

➢ **Keep moving forward.** Every step you take, no matter how small, brings you closer to your vision.

- ➢ **Keep believing in the possibility of change.** Growth happens in moments of discomfort.
- ➢ **Keep inspiring others.** Someone is watching you, learning from you, and being encouraged by the way you show up in the world.

If this book has shown you anything, I hope it is this: **You are your own superhero.** You don't need a cape or a title, **just the courage to step into who you were always meant to be.**

And as I close this message in our shared journey, **know this:**
- ✓ **Nothing is impossible.** You were built for this.
- ✓ **Every day, you have the power to say, "I'm possible."**
- ✓ **Your mission work makes the vision work.**

You've unpacked the weight. You've rewritten the narrative. You've walked through storms and discovered your purpose. Now it's time to build—with vision, with heart, and with the right people beside you. So, **keep walking, keep moving, and keep becoming.**

And never forget—**the best is yet to come.**
So, take a breath.
Stand in what you've just read.
And then, as you prepare to step into what's next take one last moment to reflect, not just where you've been, but what you're ready to build.

Because what comes next isn't just about continuing the journey…
it's about creating something that lasts.

With Love,

—Anthony Harris Brown

Now I want you to go
Live Out Loud
with No Regrets
and all heart.

Inspire Me Moment: Let's Build Something

Impact isn't just about what we create, it's about who we build with. The people we align with determine the strength of what we leave behind. Before you move ahead, consider who is helping you build and whether they are truly committed to the work.

"If you have to tell them to help carry the bricks, then they're not the ones to build with."
Coach Shaedon Meadors

Reflection:
Building something great requires more than just your vision, it requires the right people alongside you. If you constantly have to remind, beg, or convince someone to carry their share of the load, they may not be the right ones to build with.

True builders show up ready to work. They see the value in the mission, the project, or the dream, and they contribute without hesitation. They don't wait to be asked, they take initiative, bringing their own bricks, tools, and dedication.

Pay attention to who's consistently carrying weight and who's just standing by. **Build with those who build with you.**

Final Thought:
The right team doesn't need reminders; they recognize the work and show up ready to build. **Choose your builders wisely, because the strength of the foundation depends on who's laying the bricks.**

Live Out Loud Challenge: Let's Build Something

Real growth doesn't happen alone. It happens in community. But not everyone is meant to build with you. This challenge invites you to reflect on who's helping you build and how to create spaces where purpose and partnership align.

Connect

Find someone who has built something meaningful—a team, a project, a movement. Ask: *"How did you recognize the right people for your vision? What lessons did you learn about trust and collaboration?"*

Reflect

With a peer, revisit a time when you had to realign your circle or reframe a project. What shifted after the adjustment—your energy, your clarity, your momentum? How did it change your ability to walk in purpose?

Support

Challenge a mentee to audit their circle. Who's really building with them, and who's just along for the ride? Help them identify their core crew—the ones who encourage growth, model integrity, and invest in the mission too.

Wellness Check-In
Keep Walking, Keep Becoming

Purpose: You've done the work. You've unpacked the weight. You've stood in the fire and came out with vision. Now it's time to walk forward, with less fear and more intention. Before you turn the page, take a breath. This isn't the end, it's your ignition point.

Mind – One Word, One Truth

In one word, how would you describe who you are becoming?

_____

What truth about yourself is you now ready to live out loud?

_____

_____

Soul – The Silent Promise

Complete the sentence: *From this moment forward, I promise to…*

_____

_____

Now close your eyes. Say it again—with your chest.

Affirmation

"I am not finished. I am just getting started. Every step I take is building something sacred."

Repeat it. Write it. Live it.

The Inner Circle Club

**You've just stepped through something powerful.
Now it's time to speak on it and allow your "NET" Work!**

This is your space to connect, reflect, and build community with other readers.

CHAPTER 11: Keep Walking, Keep Becoming

- What does the next chapter of your life need from you?

- How do you keep believing, even when no one is clapping?

- What message do you want to leave behind for someone just beginning their journey?

EPILOGUE:
THE BECOMING CONTINUES

Becoming the Hero, You Needed

By now, you've walked the journey.

You've felt the weight of the past and the light of what's possible. You've read about a boy who once masked insecurity with charisma—and became a man who let purpose speak louder than performance.

You've seen what it means to heal in real time, to lead without a title, to rise after rejection. And you've met educators, mentors, and brothers becoming the very people they once needed.

But this isn't the end. This is your invitation.

Not just to reflect—but to respond.

Because now, it's your turn.

What Comes Next?

Take Ownership.

The breakthroughs you've seen were never about perfection—they were about alignment. Stop waiting to be told what to do. Start asking better questions about who you're becoming.

Take Action.

Legacy isn't a theory. It's built moment by moment, student by student, story by story. Let your values show up in your schedule, not just your statements.

Accept Space.

Whether you're in a classroom, a church, a living room, or a boardroom—carry your mission boldly. Speak when silence is too loud. Lead, even if your voice shakes.

You are not waiting for a hero.

You are becoming one.

Design Your Guardian Identity

Before you close this book, take a breath. And ask:

1. What pain have you repurposed into purpose?
2. Where are you called to lead—even without a title?
3. What do you carry now that your younger self once prayed for?

Write it down. Post it up.

And remember: The cape isn't out there. It's already on your back.

Final Word

As I often say:

> *"Always know that you are a Masterpiece, because you are a Piece of the Master."*

And just so you know—yeah, I used to get sent to the principal's office for talking too much. Now? I talk for a living... and became the principal I used to get sent to.

I turned my passion into purpose. My purpose into a paycheck.

And my life into a legacy.

I wasn't supposed to be the one. But God?

God specializes in using the unlikely.

So, here's your reminder:

Whatever tried to hold you back—might be the very thing pushing you forward.

You don't need a mic to be anointed.

You don't need applause to be impactful.

You just need to say yes—and stand.

Keep talking. Keep teaching. Keep becoming.

The work is working.

Now let it work through you.

> *So, whether you're holding a clipboard, a mic, a journal, or just the weight of your story—know this: your calling is already calling. Now it's your turn to answer. No regrets. All heart.*

Inspire Me Moment:
Is the Anger Worth It?

There's power in knowing what to hold onto and what to let go of. Anger, if left unchecked, can be a heavy weight to carry. But when released, it makes space for clarity, peace, and forward movement. Before stepping into what's next, consider: Is the anger worth it?

"Holding on to anger is like drinking poison and expecting the other person to die."
Buddha

Here is the first ever moment that started it all. After weeks of just posting graphics and quotes on social media, this was the first video post. Who knew it would lead to something bigger.

Reflection:
Anger is a heavy thing to carry. It doesn't just sit quietly in the background—it festers, grows, and takes up space in your mind, body, and soul. Holding onto anger, resentment, or past pain only hurts you, not the person you're mad at. So why let it stay?

State your case. Speak your truth. Find peace with it. And then let it go. Because while you're out here holding onto bitterness, the world is still moving. And you? You've got bigger and better things to do.

Final Thought:
Anger only holds power over you if you let it. Release it, reflect on it, and move forward with a renewed sense of peace. Don't let anger keep you from reaching the next step in your journey.

Live Out Loud Challenge:
Is the Anger Worth It?

Anger is real and sometimes righteous, but it's meant to be a visitor, not a tenant. This challenge invites you to honor your emotions but not let them hold your future hostage.

Connect

Reach out to someone you admire who has turned pain into peace. Ask: **What helped you move from anger to action? How did releasing it strengthen—not weaken—you?**

Reflect

With a trusted peer, share a time when holding onto anger that cost you something important—time, peace, relationships, opportunities. What shifted when you finally let it go? What could shift now if you choose peace again?

Support

Encourage a younger peer or mentee to see forgiveness and release as tools of strength, not surrender. Share a personal moment where letting go freed you to build something better.

Movement is medicine. Track your progress, celebrate your wins, and stay connected to the strength you're building inside and out.

FITNESS PLANNER

DATE: _____   S   M   T   W   T   F   S

GOALS OF THE DAY

- ◉ ☐ _____
- ◉ ☐ _____
- ◉ ☐ _____
- ◉ ☐ _____

	WORKOUT	TIME	REPS
◉ ☐			
◉ ☐			
◉ ☐			
◉ ☐			
◉ ☐			
◉ ☐			
◉ ☐			
◉ ☐			
◉ ☐			
◉ ☐			
◉ ☐			
◉ ☐			
◉ ☐			
◉ ☐			
◉ ☐			

WATER INTAKE

◌ ◌ ◌ ◌   ◌ ◌ ◌ ◌   ◌ ◌
1 L   2 L   3 L

TODAY'S MOOD

☺ ☹ ☺ ☹ ☹ ☺ ☹

DAILY NUTRITION

Breakfast _____

Lunch _____

Dinner _____

Snacks _____

TODAY I'M GRATEFUL FOR

_____

_____

_____

◉ TO START   ⊘ OK   ⊖ DELAY   ⊘ STUCK   ⊗ CANCEL

Pause. Breathe. Look within. Use this space to unpack the day—what moved you, challenged you, or taught you. Every moment holds meaning.

Daily Reflection Journal

Date _____ / _____ / _____

Mood Tracker

Choose a face

Add a description _____

_____

_____

Highlights of the day

01	
02	
03	
04	
05	
06	
07	

Gratitude List

What I learned today

Goals for tomorrow

ACKNOWLEDGMENTS

Writing *Inspire Me Moments: Living Out Loud with No Regrets* was never a solo act. Every step of this journey was touched, strengthened, and inspired by the incredible people who surrounded me with encouragement, truth, and heart.

First and foremost, I thank God for being my constant source of strength, wisdom, and inspiration. Without His grace and favor, none of this would be possible.

To my team of trusted editors, reviewers, and advisors – thank you for your thoughtful feedback, late-night conversations, and commitment to helping me bring this vision to life. Your belief in the power of these words fueled me in the hard days and sharpened the message on the good ones.

To the published authors, educators, leaders, and everyday heroes who offered your insight – your voices helped shape these pages into something bigger than me.

To my family, friends, and community – you are my why. Thank you for walking with me through every season, cheering for me in the quiet moments when no one else was watching, and reminding me that love, faith, and purpose are more powerful than any obstacle.

To every reader who picks up this book, you are now part of this story. I hope that as you turned these pages, you found your own reflections, your own courage, and your own call to action.

Bonus Invitation:

If this book speaks to you, I invite you to connect. Visit **www.AHarrisBrown.com** or tag me on social media. Let's keep walking, growing, and living out loud together.

With deep gratitude and much love,

Anthony H. Brown

REFERENCES

American College Health Association. (2023). American College Health Association-National College Health Assessment III: Undergraduate student reference group executive summary, Spring 2023. https://www.acha.org/documents/ncha/NCHA-III_SPRING_2023_US_REFERENCE_GROUP_EXECUTIVE_SUMMARY.pdf

American Foundation for Suicide Prevention. (2023). *Suicide statistics.* https://afsp.org/suicide-statistics

American Psychiatric Association. (2022). Mental health disparities: African Americans. https://www.psychiatry.org/psychiatrists/cultural-competency/education/mental-health-facts

Baum, L. F. (1900). The wonderful wizard of Oz. George M. Hill Company.

Brown, B. (2012). Daring greatly: How the courage to be vulnerable transforms the way we live, love, parent, and lead. Gotham Books.

Hammond, W. P. (2012). Taking it like a man: Masculine role norms as moderators of the racial discrimination–depressive symptoms association among African American men. American Journal of Public Health, 102(S2), S232–S241. https://doi.org/10.2105/AJPH.2011.300485

hooks, b. (2000). *All about love: New visions*. William Morrow.

Lumet, S. (Director). (1978). *The Wiz* [Film]. Universal Pictures.

Mahalik, J. R., Burns, S. M., & Syzdek, M. (2003). Masculinity and perceived normative health behaviors as predictors of men's health behaviors. Social Science & Medicine, 64(11), 2201–2209. https://doi.org/10.1016/S0277-9536(02)00403-4

Mayo Clinic Staff. (2024). *Gastric bypass (Roux-en-Y)*. Mayo Clinic. https://www.mayoclinic.org/tests-procedures/gastric-bypass/about/pac-20384555

Movember Foundation. (2018, October 31). *Men's health survey*. https://uk.movember.com/story/view/id/11740/men-s-health-survey

National Alliance on Mental Illness. (n.d.). Support and education. https://www.nami.org/Support-Education

National Institute on Alcohol Abuse and Alcoholism. (n.d.). *Alcohol facts and statistics*. U.S. Department of Health and Human Services, National Institutes of Health. https://www.niaaa.nih.gov/alcohols-effects-health/alcohol-facts-and-statistics

National Institute of Mental Health. (2023). Mental illness. U.S. Department of Health and Human Services. https://www.nimh.nih.gov/health/statistics/mental-illness

Prostate Cancer Foundation. (2024). Prostate cancer in Black men. https://www.pcf.org/about-prostate-cancer/black-men-and-prostate-cancer/

Zondervan. (2011). *Holy Bible: New International Version*. (Original work published 1973).

RESOURCES

The following resources provide support, guidance, and opportunities that align with the themes explored in this book. Whether you are looking for mental health support, mentorship, career development, family engagement, HBCU support, or faith-based inspiration, these organizations and platforms offer tools to help you navigate your journey.

🪓 Mental Health & Emotional Wellness

- American Foundation for Suicide Prevention
  https://afsp.org/

- Psychology Today – Find a Therapist
  https://www.psychologytoday.com/us

- National Alliance on Mental Illness (NAMI)
  https://www.nami.org

- Therapy for Black Men
  https://www.therapyforblackmen.org

- Black Mental Wellness
  https://www.blackmentalwellness.com

- BEAM (Black Emotional and Mental Health Collective)
  https://www.beam.community

- The Safe Place App
  Available on iOS & Android

- GriefShare – Faith-Based Grief Support
  https://www.griefshare.org

- Black Men Heal
  https://www.blackmenheal.org

- The Confess Project
  https://www.theconfessproject.com

- Boris L. Henson Foundation
  https://www.borislhensonfoundation.org

- Steve Fund
  https://www.stevefund.org

- Brother, You're on My Mind
  https://www.nimhd.nih.gov/programs/edu-training/byomm/

✑ Substance Abuse & Addiction Recovery

- Alcoholics Anonymous (AA)
  https://www.aa.org

- Substance Abuse and Mental Health Services Administration
  https://www.samhsa.gov

- SMART Recovery
  https://www.smartrecovery.org

- Black Mental Health Alliance
  https://www.blackmentalhealth.com

- NIDA – Men's Addiction Recovery Resources
  https://www.drugabuse.gov

- National Institute on Alcohol Abuse and Alcoholism (NIAAA)
  https://www.niaaa.nih.gov

✑ Faith, Healing & Spiritual Growth

- Our Daily Bread Ministries
  https://www.odb.org

- HBCU Faith & Leadership Institute
  https://www.hbcufaithleadership.org

- NAMI FaithNet
  https://www.nami.org/FaithNet

- The King Center – Beloved Community Resources
  https://www.thekingcenter.org

- Bible App (YouVersion)
  https://www.youversion.com

- Faith & Prejudice
  https://www.faithandprejudice.com

🔨 HBCU-Specific Resources

- Common Black College Application (CBCA)
  https://www.commonblackcollegeapp.com

- United Negro College Fund (UNCF)
  https://www.uncf.org

- Thurgood Marshall College Fund (TMCF)
  https://www.tmcf.org

- HBCU First
  https://www.hbcufirst.com

- The HBCU Foundation
  https://www.thehbcufoundation.org

- Bethune-Cookman University
  https://www.cookman.edu

- Clark Atlanta University
  https://www.cau.edu

- The HBCU Digest
  https://www.hbcudigest.com

- The Center for Minority Serving Institutions
  https://www.gse.upenn.edu/cmsi

🔨 Weight Loss & Health Transformation

- Obesity Action Coalition (OAC)
  https://www.obesityaction.org

- American Society for Metabolic and Bariatric Surgery (ASMBS)
  https://www.asmbs.org

- ObesityHelp.com
  https://www.obesityhelp.com

- Black Women's Health Imperative
  https://www.bwhi.org

📌 Family Engagement & Community Support

- Ohio Statewide Family Engagement Center
  https://www.ohiofamiliesengage.osu.edu

- National Fatherhood Initiative (NFI)
  https://www.fatherhood.org

- Black Family Development, Inc.
  https://www.blackfamilydevelopment.org

- National PTA – Engagement Programs
  https://www.pta.org

- Fathers Incorporated
  https://www.fathersincorporated.com

- Urban Strategies Inc.
  https://www.urbanstrategies.org

📌 Leadership, Advocacy & Purpose

- Profound Gentlemen
  https://www.profoundgentlemen.org

- Code M Magazine
  https://www.codemmagazine.com

- New Leaders – National Aspiring Principals Fellowship
  https://www.newleaders.org

- National Equity Project
  https://www.nationalequityproject.org

- The Brotherhood Sister Sol
  https://www.brotherhood-sistersol.org

- The Hidden Genius Project
  https://www.hiddengeniusproject.org

- Restorative Justice for Oakland Youth (RJOY)
  https://www.rjoyoakland.org

- Call Me MISTER
  https://www.callmemister.com

🪓 Men's Health, Mental Wellness & Brotherhood

- American Heart Association – Blood Pressure Info
  https://www.heart.org/hbp

- Colorectal Cancer Alliance
  https://www.ccalliance.org

- Prostate Cancer Foundation
  https://www.pcf.org

- Movember Foundation – Men's Health
  https://us.movember.com/

- Black Mental Health Alliance
  https://www.blackmentalhealth.com

- I Am Man Enough
  https://manenough.com

These resources are here to support your **mental, emotional, spiritual, and professional journey**. No matter where you're starting from—you don't have to walk it alone.

Use them. Share them. Build with them.

REFLECTION INDEX

Use this guide to revisit key reflections and turn insight into action. Each chapter concludes with a powerful set of tools to help you process, connect, and grow. These aren't just bonus pages, they're the heartbeat of this journey. Here's where you'll find them:

WHAT ARE THE PEOPLE SAYING...

"Inspire Me Moments" is one of the most profound books I've had the pleasure of reading in a long time. He gets naked in his truth and then provides you with a place to share your truths. The journey that the author takes you on is refreshing. The world needed this!

Melvin White
Founder/President
Frat Dads LLC

"Inspire Me Moments" met me where my grief lived, in the thick silence between pain and the possibility of release. A. Harris Brown doesn't just write. He reaches into your heart and hands you back the pieces you thought were lost. You won't be disappointed!

Ms. Tyler Hughley, M. Ed.
Humanware Partner
Cleveland Metropolitan School District

You're the author of your own story, therefore my friend, write well…

Donté R. Harris
Guidance Counselor
Charlotte Mecklenburg Schools

A great journey, with a wonderful ending. Take the trip that this book takes you on and you will not regret the process!!

Dr. Kalvin Wall
Associate Director
North Carolina Dept. of Health and Human Services

"Inspire Me Moments" is a reminder that life isn't just about how we arrive, it's about trusting the journey, lifting others while we climb, and realizing the power to create legacy has always been within us.

Roger Gray, IV
Admissions Counselor
Tuskegee University

I'm inspired by this movement as it has truly blessed me as I've dealt with many of the situations in this book. Thanks for providing a valuable resource to everyone who reads this masterpiece.

Dr. Monique Robinson
CEO/Founder
A Better Chance for Youth Futures Inc.

I'm truly honored to get a sneak peek of the powerful book he's put together, and I'm excited for the many people his story will encourage, inspire, and impact. That's a rare quality and one I deeply respect.

Wayne N. Terrell, Jr.
Senior Impact Manager
Profound Another Look Television Show

"Inspire Me Moments" is more than a book, it's a testament to perseverance, purpose, and personal growth. It's a must-read for anyone ready to stop making excuses and start making moves.

Maurice Jordan
Creator
The HBCU Trivia Game

The most inspiring leaders allow their harshest tests to become the most beautiful testimony They allow their breakthrough to become someone else's blueprint. Anthony poured his heart out in a way that will inspire, challenge, and provoke change in the heart of the readers. This is a book you must read.

Maurice F. Martin
Transformational Coach and Author
Total Harmony Leadership Solutions

Whether Anthony Brown knows it or not, he has always been larger than life and not speaking to size but to personality and influence. His "journey" deserves to be shared with the world for others to benefit from an example of perseverance despite all odds, you can make it!!!

Dr. Linda Woodard
President
LDW Group LLC

One of the most talented and versatile individuals I have ever met. I am truly delighted that his journey, life experiences, and career will be shared with the world. I plan to purchase several copies of "Inspire Me Moments," for its inspirational, motivational, and educational value to share with all my family and friends.

Jeffrey J. Phelps
Producer/Director
Another Look Television Show

I am so proud and honored to be a part of A. Harris Brown's life. He has always been an inspiration to me. I saw him grow from a young man to an adult, and I'm so honored to have been there to see his growth and his change.

Robert Starks
Teacher
New York City Department of Education

Reading the section, The Times My Father Changed My Life, made me reflect deeply on my relationship with my own father and brother. Thank you, Anthony, for inspiring connection, reflection, and support. Your words ignite something powerful in my journey.

Danielle Williams
Member
PHA-OES & National Sorority of Phi Delta Kappa, Inc.

This book peel back the layers of trauma and self-doubt that many men struggle with in silence. My hope is that other men will read this book and find the courage and strength to live again.

Keith Langford
Family and Community Engagement Supervisor
Shaker Heights City School District

In a world full of chaos and adversity, Anthony has shown us that when life throws daggers at you and tries to throw you off your game, you must KEEP GOING. Anthony has written more than just a book; he's created a 101 guide on how to master adversity like a champion.

Adrena Martin
Founder
Historically Black Since

Anthony H. Brown has crafted a true masterpiece. His honesty and openness in sharing his life story are both powerful and inspiring. This work is sure to resonate deeply with readers. If you're in search of encouragement or motivation, this is a must read.

George Sanders
Founder/CEO
Daily Gospel Network

Anthony has proven to be a quintessential authority on HBCUs and his commitment to communities of color is unsurpassed. His voice and transparency are unparalleled, and his life has been nothing but a miracle.

Robert Mason
Founder/CEO
The Common Black College Application

ABOUT THE AUTHOR

Anthony Harris Brown is a visionary leader, educator, minister, media personality, and community advocate dedicated to empowering students, families, and educators through faith, storytelling, and service. Raised in a resilient urban community, Anthony overcame significant challenges, including a major health scare, depression, and a 200+ pound weight loss journey that shaped his passion for servant leadership and educational equity.

With over 25 years in education, he serves as the Family and Community Engagement Program Manager for the Cleveland Metropolitan School District and holds an Alternative Principal License. He is a graduate of the Clark Atlanta University/New Leaders National Aspiring Principals Fellowship and leads the CMSD MOCHA Network, focused on mentoring and keeping Black male educators.

Anthony serves as Minister of Worship and Arts at Second New Hope Missionary Baptist Church in Cleveland, where he blends faith, creativity, and compassion. He is also the host of The HBCU Alumni House Party Show and co-host of The HBCU Man Cave podcast—platforms that celebrate Black excellence, leadership, and wellness.

A proud HBCU graduate and former President of the UNCF National Alumni Council, Anthony's legacy includes the creation of the Anthony H. Brown HBCU Arts Scholarship.

His journey is a living testimony to his personal mantra:
Live Loud. Lead Bold. Love Deep.

My mission is to instill a desire for growth by living an exemplary life as an effective and exceptional father, friend, educator, leader, artist and supporter to those that shall cross my path in life.

Always know that you are a Masterpiece, because you are a Piece of the Master.

Visit the website or scan QR Code to Savings

Scan QR Code for More Information